HIDDEN
WARWICKSHIRE

HIDDEN
WARWICKSHIRE

Betty Smith

with illustrations by Pip Challenger

COUNTRYSIDE BOOKS
NEWBURY, BERKSHIRE

COUNTRYSIDE BOOKS
3 Catherine Road
Newbury, Berkshire

ISBN 1 85306 098 4

Front cover photograph of Tredington
taken by Andy Williams
Back cover photograph of Folly Tower, Idlicote
taken by Victor Smith

Produced through MRM Associates Ltd., Reading
Printed in England by J. W. Arrowsmith Ltd., Bristol

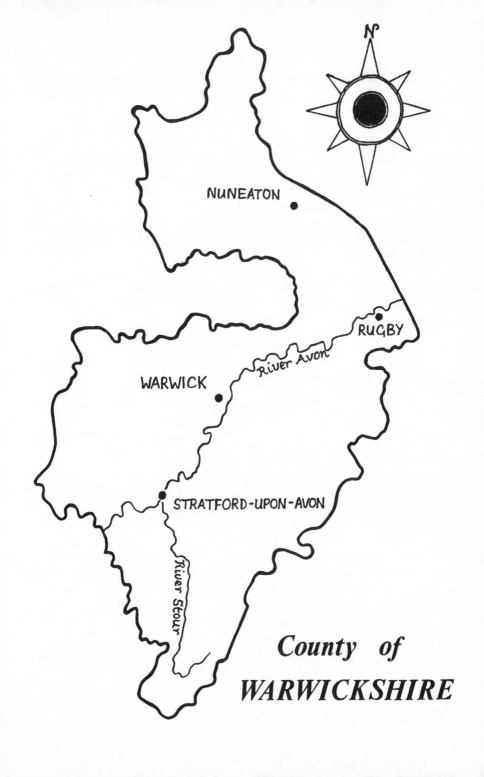

N

NUNEATON

RUGBY

River Avon

WARWICK

STRATFORD-UPON-AVON

River Stour

County of
WARWICKSHIRE

Introduction

The county of Warwickshire lies right in the centre of England; the very heart of the country, as it is so often called. Warwickshire is a county of immense contrasts, with areas of great beauty.

In the deep south of the county, where its boundaries nudge the Cotswolds, the villages have taken upon themselves something of a Cotswold character. The undulating hills, gentle slopes rising not more than a few hundred feet are where the Wolds begin, and the older buildings with their mullioned windows and sun-warmed stone are archetypal Cotswold.

On the Oxfordshire borders, villages present a sterner aspect as the native ironstone darkens, and are much more working communities. To the north of the Avon valley, rich in waterways, lakes and canals, lie villages whose industrial heritage has given them an enviable sense of community.

Because of its position, Warwickshire has seen much history. It seems that everyone marching from north to south and vice versa must have come through our county. Battles have been fought, not only of the bloody kind, but the industrial variety as well. Notable people have had their exits and their entrances upon our stage. Warwick the Kingmaker marched from his great castle in the county town; Queen Elizabeth I seemed to find pleasure in travelling through Warwick and enjoying many entertainments, and her great favourite, the Earl of Leicester, an ambitious man, regularly entertained her in Warwickshire. We have bred Michael Drayton, George Eliot, and, of course, Shakespeare, whose works so accurately reflect the Warwickshire of his day and age.

Ancient traditions still abound in Warwickshire. We still hold the mop fairs, a left-over from the days when servants and farm labourers went to the fair, carrying a symbol of their calling, ie a whip for a carter; sheep's wool on a crook for a shepherd; a dish mop for a maid servant; a pail for a milkmaid, and got looked over by potential employers before being hired for the following year. They had an opportunity to leave, should all not prove satisfactory, for at Stratford, ten days after the Mop, is the 'Runaway Mop' where servants could run away from unsatisfactory employment, and get taken on by another master.

Born and bred in Warwickshire, I thought I knew my native heath pretty well; but my travels in search of 'Hidden' Warwickshire have taken me to places unfamiliar to me. In every village there is a story. As a journalist, there is nothing I enjoy more than a good story. Describing villages is not easy, for almost all have interesting buildings; bits of architecture; trees, ponds and village greens There is no village anywhere that doesn't have a point of specific interest, but it is the stories of those who once lived there that fascinate me. I have spent many hours on my knees in churchyards attempting to decipher a well worn headstone and many further hours trying to unravel the story behind the inscription. Not always with success, I must confess, for record keeping in the past was not as carefully undertaken as it is today.

Given a vivid imagination, it is a simple matter to conjure up a visual image of how ancient people lived and details of their daily life; of the man or woman behind the odd inscription upon their headstone.

In the months I have researched 'Hidden Warwickshire' I have travelled all over my own county. Most of the places have found their way into this book; some of them haven't! It has been necessary to be selective, and I have tried to use the more unusual aspects, and naturally those that specifically interested me.

Now, though, I have quite a few places to add to my already long list of personal favourites. I hope you will add them to yours.

Betty Smith

Acknowledgements

I am indebted to the staff of the Warwickshire County Record Office, and the Shakespeare Birthplace Trust Record Office, for their help. To the staff of the County Museum, and the Warwick Library; to the staff of our local library at Shipston-on-Stour who made records available to me, and obtained the many books I persistently requested.

I am grateful to all those people I met on my travels who took time to tell me stories and point out to me items I might otherwise have missed.

I am especially grateful to all those people who have written notes upon their church and village, sometimes in the form of booklets to be purchased, or merely notes pinned upon the church notice board. These are not only useful, but usually jolly interesting as well.

I am especially grateful to my husband, Victor Smith, who accompanied me on many of my travels, helped with researches, read copy, and took hundreds of photographs, all with great patience!

Alcocks Arbour

Between the lovely little village of Kinwarton in the valley of the Alne and the nearby village of Haselor is a prominent hill covered with trees which has earned for itself the name of Alcocks Arbour. And thereby hangs a tale, the origins of which are lost in the mists of antiquity. Even Dugdale, writing in 1656 (*Antiquities of Warwickshire*) could throw little light upon the subject.

It seems that at the foot of Alcocks Arbour there used to be the entrance to a cave, quite a small hole, which led to a large chamber. A man called Alcock lived within the cave and earned his daily bread by robbery. So adept was he that the spoils of his raids rapidly filled the large chamber in which he made his home. So much money did Alcock accumulate that he had to get a large iron bound chest to contain it. The chest had three separate locks and three keys, and upon it sat a cock as a guard.

Like everyone else, Alcock eventually died, but the cock lived on, still sitting on top of the vast chest of money. One day a learned scholar came to look into this legend of Alcock's Arbour, and brought with him various keys. Apparently he managed to open two of the locks, and thought he might even manage the third, but the great cock seized him, and thwarted his efforts. Alcock's body was never found, and the legend goes on to state that if you can produce a bone of the man that set the cock upon his long vigil, then the secret of the chest shall be yours.

That is the legend. Much later, it was decided among experts that the mound itself is the tomb of a Celtic chief named Olcobhar. So the secret in this case is more likely to be the true entrance to the cave, where the great chief was probably buried with all his armour and weapons.

Only about 500 yards from this spot is a spring bearing the name Caldwell and here it is believed once stood a hermitage, the traces of which have long since disappeared. Could it be that the hermit simply didn't want to be bothered by visitors, and invented the story of the great cock? Or perhaps he even buried a bit of treasure himself, and decided that a good legend was the best possible defence against thieves.

Arlescote

This really is a hidden part of the county, tucked just below the Edgehill escarpment, approached by a narrow turning off Knole End and down a winding lane which leads out ultimately towards the Dassett Hills.

Arlescote is a hamlet, a mere handful of houses and farms, clutching at the gentle wooded slopes and clustered around the venerable manor house, once the lodging of two Royal princes. The house was built in Tudor times, and curious window fastenings were fashioned. These, when open, form the letters 'ER' believed by their dating to stand for 'Edwardus Rex'.

In October 1642 the first battle of the Civil War took place on the flat lands below the Edge hills. King Charles I was on his way to Oxford with his two sons, the princes Charles and James, when Lord Essex and his Parliamentarian troops marched through the night to halt the Royalist army. The young princes, with their tutor William Harvey, were sent for safety to lodge at the manor house, Arlescote, while their father attended to his more pressing engagement.

William Harvey was already a distinguished physician, and renowned for his work on the discovery of the circulation of blood round the human body. He was in attendance upon the King, not only to render medical aid, but also to take charge of the twelve year old Charles, and nine year old James.

The boys fretted at not being allowed anywhere near the battle, and at length William Harvey took them up to the top of the rise that they might look down upon the plain below. The ever studious Harvey sat down upon the grass, and taking a book from his pocket, began to read. Quite suddenly a shot was fired and the musket ball seared the page of the book, narrowly missing him. The battle had begun!

Harvey bustled the young princes back into the safety of the manor house, and kept them indoors. Charles, at an age when boredom comes easy, chafed at this confinement and gazed out of the window, seeing nothing but the gardens, and yet hearing the sound of cannon. Taking a ring from his finger he idly scratched 'Charles' and the date, with the diamond upon the pane of glass.

The manor house came into the hands of the Goodwin family, landowners hereabouts, and thence by marriage into the Taylor Loder family of Williamscote. The pane of glass was removed for safekeeping when the house was altered by Inigo Jones in the 17th century, and when last heard of, it still remained in the hands of the Taylor Loders.

Behind the manor is an old pond which, according to local tradition, has two outlets, one of which flows into the Avon and thence to the Severn, whilst the other goes into the Cherwell and ends up in the Thames.

An amusing story is told of Arlescote House at the beginning of the 19th century, when a Mr Holloway who lived there was the Captain of the Kineton Volunteers, and a very enthusiastic one. The company had a field day, and afterwards when the muskets were handed in, one of them was found to be full of cartridges from butt to nozzle. The man was sent for, and questioned, and it appeared that he had assiduously loaded up on the command, but when the word was given to 'fire' his nerve failed him and he couldn't bring himself to pull the trigger. Fortunately, perhaps, the Kineton Volunteers were never called upon for active service.

About one mile from the old manor house is Nadbury Camp, an old Iron Age fortification, of which not much remains. Quite a lot of archaeological work has been done on this site, revealing many skeletons, together with weapons, a brass sword and a battleaxe.

Armscote

➤ The traveller may well think he has passed through Armscote, and indeed he has, upon the road that skirts the main part of the village. But he is unlikely ever to pass through the older part of this small and secluded hamlet. This part lines a loop road, and unless you had reason to penetrate the inner reaches, then you haven't really seen Armscote.

It has old stone houses and mellow stone walls, leading towards a village pond, but its greatest claim to fame is the old Quaker meeting house well hidden behind hedges and trees, where George Fox was arrested. It was not at that time (1673) a proper meeting house. It was a barn, but was built into a meeting house in 1680.

George Fox was a visionary, and walked the length and breadth of the countryside preaching. Basically, in Fox's philosophy, Quakers would not accept any organised religion; would not use titles; would not remove their hats except in the presence of God; would not swear oaths, and would not keep what they considered to be pagan festivals. Obviously this kind of preaching was an anathema to the established order of the Church, and there was concern about the spread of Quakerism in South Warwickshire.

At that time, some vicars were not very assiduous in their duties and often lived miles away from the living whence came their income, or part of it. Such a one was Josephus Crowther of nearby Tredington, who held so many Church offices and neglected his parochial duties so shamefully that he was universally held in contempt. Sir Henry Parker was lord of the manor at Honington, and involved himself much in Church affairs. Rowland Arris, who had purchased both honours and qualifications, became eventually vicar of Honington. To do him credit, though, he did carry out his parochial duties with scrupulous attention, but was of necessity under the thumb of Sir Henry Parker. These three men knew of George Fox and his teachings, and decided to act against the man himself.

They heard of the impending visit of George Fox from a wet nurse employed in the Parker household at Honington. Fox was on his way back to his native heath in Lancashire, and stopped overnight at Adderbury in Oxfordshire, where a meeting of worship was held.He had a premonition of danger, but because he feared no one except the Lord, he, his wife, daughter and son-in-law, Thomas Lower, walked on from Adderbury to Armscote, where a meeting of worship was held in a barn belonging to John Halford, a local lawyer. Fox preached, and was welcomed.

The meeting was over, and Fox and his family were in the nearby house of a friend taking refreshment before again setting off on their journey, when Parker, Crowther and Arris arrived. They burst in and arrested Fox and Thomas Lower, and took both of them to Worcester gaol.

There was really no case to answer, although there was much acrimonious argument, particularly from Sir Henry Parker, who claimed that George Fox and those who followed him had emptied the local churches, to the detriment of the parsons. Thomas Lower was at pains to point out that the parsons seldom carried out their proper duties anyway, and if they had been doing so, then the people would not have left church and gone to hear George Fox instead!

Josephus Crowther threatened to sue Lower for defamation, but realising from the laughter within the court that many there knew the allegation to be true, he never did so. Sir Henry Parker ranted and raved, and said that Fox was stirring up his followers into revolution against the King. Fox and Lower remained in prison for some months whilst the arguments raged back and forth, but eventually they were released.

The Quaker meeting house at Armscote remains, but is only used once a year now, on the first Sunday in every August.

Arrow

From the nearby busy market town of Alcester the river Arrow meanders south, and gives its name to the small hamlet on the route towards Evesham. There is not much left of Arrow now, except a group of old black and white cottages once the homes of farm workers, and now much restored and modernised. They are close to an old toll house which must have been kept busy in the old turnpike days.

On the opposite side of the road, and down a long and winding field road, the church stands near the river. It has a plain Norman doorway, and a tower designed in the 18th century by Horace Walpole who was a frequent visitor to nearby Ragley Park, home of the Marquis of Hertford.

The church was restored in 1863, when a stone coffin lid was discovered. This, now in the church, dates from 1303, and is from the casket of Sir Gerard de Camville, who fought with Edward I in Scotland. The Camvilles held these lands for many years, but Sir Gerard had only one child, Elizabeth, who was sought in marriage by her cousin, Henry de Camville. The girl was under age, and sometime about 1312 Henry complained to the King, Edward II, that a Robert Burdet, assisted by others, had forcibly abducted her from her home at Arrow. By the time the truth was discovered, Elizabeth was legally married to Robert Burdet, and the lands of the Camvilles came to him.

Thomas Burdet owned it in 1477, during the reign of Edward IV, but the King was bit suspicious of Thomas because of his friendship with the Duke of Clarence. Edward decided to go hunting at Arrow, and during a good day's sport, he killed a white buck in Arrow Park. The King was well pleased. But Thomas Burdet was not. When he returned, and was told the King had killed his favourite buck, the one he was keeping for himself, he flew into a passion and loudly declared he wished the beast had put its horns in the King's belly. There were many loyal sycophants around all too ready to repeat this into the ear of the King, and as a consequence Thomas Burdet was charged with high treason, summarily tried and rapidly hanged.

Thomas Burdet had divorced his first wife, Agnes, by whom he had a son, Richard. He had married again, and had another son by his second wife. The son by his second marriage, John Burdet, was made his sole heir and the son of the first marriage, Richard, was totally disinherited. On his way to be hanged at Tyburn, Thomas Burdet espied his son Richard in the crowd waiting to witness the hanging. He spoke to Richard, asking him to forgive the great wrong he had done to him and his mother, for which he was being punished. Richard took out a law suit against his half brother John, which went on for some 20 or more years. By the time it was resolved, they were both long gone.

On the south side of the church is a recumbent effigy in white marble of Admiral Sir George Francis Seymour who died in 1870. This was erected by his son Francis, the 5th Marquis of Hertford, and is the work of his son-in-law, the late Prince Hohenlohe, better known as Count Gleichen, nephew of Queen Victoria, who ran away to sea, and then gave up the sea for his art, in which he was greatly encouraged by his Royal aunt.

A short walk away is Arrow Mill, now a restaurant but once very much a working mill, mentioned in the Domesday survey, and in the hands of the Sisam family for more than a century. The mill wheel still turns, although now it is enclosed and forms a talking point inside the hotel.

Astley

A completely unselfconscious little village in the midst of George Eliot country, for Astley is the 'Knebley' of *Mr Gilfil's Love Story*, and Robert and Christiana Evans, the parents of Mary Ann Evans who took the pen name George Eliot, were married at Astley church. Her aunt, Mrs Ann Garner, who was portrayed as one of the Dodson sisters in *Mill on the Floss*, lived at Astley and is buried in the churchyard.

It is an estate village, the neat houses and flat green fields clustered around the collegiate church of St Mary the Virgin, a truly remarkable church and in my view one of the most rewarding in the entire county. It was founded by Sir Thomas Astley in 1343 as a college for priests, and although it has suffered many vicissitudes, like all our churches, it still has an air of sombre majesty. It has superb painted stalls, 18 out of a set of 24. Those on the north side are the apostles, and upon the south the prophets. There are painted panels with strap work patterns, dating from the 17th century. There are misericords, and monuments with a quaint turn of phrase, notably one to Lettice Bolton, who, it is said lived 'very handsomely upon a narrow fortune. Her life was without trouble, and her death without pain' when she 'expired suddenly' on 17th February 1693 at the age of 65.

Astley castle ruins

But the real story of Astley concerns two sad Queens of England. Behind the church and across fields are the remains of Astley Castle, a fortified manor house first built by Philip Astley in 1170, and then rebuilt around 1555. It was originally a Saxon homestead moat, one of the 150 that were strewn throughout Warwickshire.

The castle came into the hands of the Grey family, and Sir John Grey married a beautiful lady called Elizabeth Woodville. They had two sons, and then Sir John was killed fighting for the mad King Henry VI at the Battle of St Albans in 1461, and Elizabeth was left a desolate widow. She is believed to have lived at Astley in the early years of her widowhood, but because much of the Grey estates had been seized, she had little upon which to live.

Hearing that the new King, Edward IV, often hunted in Grafton forest just over the Northamptonshire border, Elizabeth Woodville went to stay with her mother at Grafton, and one day, taking her two infant sons by the hand, she awaited the King beneath an oak tree. When he rode near, she cast herself at his feet and begged him to restore their father's lands to her two sons.

16

Elizabeth was a beautiful woman, and the King was very susceptible. He fell in love with her and married her, to the great consternation of his court. They had two sons and seven daughters, but the poor Queen lost her sons upon the death of their father. The little boys were thrown into the Tower from whence they never emerged. It is argued they were murdered upon the instructions of their 'wicked' uncle, Richard III, but there are those who believe the instructions are more likely to have come from the new King, Henry VII, the victor of Bosworth field. In order to strengthen his tenuous claim to the throne, he thought it politic to marry Elizabeth's eldest daughter, the Princess Elizabeth of York. Elizabeth Woodville, once Queen of England, died destitute of personal possessions at Whitsuntide in 1492, and is buried with King Edward IV at Windsor.

The other sad Queen who lived at Astley was Lady Jane Grey, daughter of Henry Lord Grey and his wife, the Lady Frances, eldest daughter of Charles Brandon Duke of Suffolk. In the absence of male heirs to the title, Edward VI created Henry Grey Duke of Suffolk. Suffolk was an ambitious man, and was as thick as thieves with the Duke of Northumberland, equally ambitious. To cement the relationship, Lady Jane was married to Guilford Dudley, son of the Duke of Northumberland.

Northumberland almost ruled the country through the sickly little boy King, but constantly sought more power. When the King died, Suffolk, urged on by Northumberland, declared his daughter Lady Jane Grey, Queen of England.

Poor little gentle Jane, only 17 years old, unworldly, pious, and learned beyond her years, had no wish to be Queen, but she and her young husband had to do as they were told. Little Jane was 'Queen for Nine Days'. Then Mary Tudor marched into London, and promptly threw Jane and Guilford Dudley into the Tower. They were beheaded upon Tower Hill on 12th February 1554. Suffolk himself was released when his wife, Lady Frances, cousin to Queen Mary, begged for his life.

He didn't learn his lesson. Almost at once he involved himself in Sir Thomas Wyatt's plot against the Queen's marriage to Philip of Spain, and came into Warwickshire to stir up sedition. The whole rebellion was a rapid failure and Suffolk fled to Astley to evade capture.

Here he took refuge in an old hollow tree in the park at Astley and remained hidden for four days, looked after by one of his keepers, a man called Underwood, who brought him food. But every man has his price, they say, and when Underwood was offered money to betray his master, he did so. Suffolk was dragged from his hollow oak, and lost his head upon Tower Hill on 23rd February 1554.

The Lady Frances wasted no time mourning either her husband or her daughter, and within three weeks married her equerry, Adrian Stokes. He doesn't seem to have been a very nice man, and as soon as he got to Astley he began defacing the church, stripping every bit of lead off the roof and spire. The estate came into the hands of the Chamberlain family in 1558, and in 1600 the great spire of the church, a landmark for miles around, referred to as 'the lanthorn of Arden' collapsed, having no lead to protect it.

The Chamberlains began to rebuild the church in 1607. According to Dugdale's *Antiquities of Warwickshire* this involved the pulling down of side chapels, and the removal of beautiful alabaster effigies to Sir Thomas Grey and his wife. Dugdale tells us he was present when their coffins were discovered beneath the alabaster. 'By the curious desire of some', he says, 'the coffins were opened'. The bodies were discovered, wrapped in 'cerecloth' which was also cut open. The corpses were found to be absolutely perfect, even though they had been buried for almost 80 years. It was decided to set the effigies up again, but according to Dugdale, this was not done, and they were thrown into an outhouse with a lot of rubbish.

There are three effigies still within the church, and it is just possible to imagine what Lady Jane Grey might have looked like, for these are her ancestors — Sir Edward Grey, died 1457, Elizabeth Talbot, wife of Edward Grey, Lord Lisle, died 1483, and the beautiful Cecily Bonnville, wife of Thomas Grey, Marquess of Dorset. They are small, fine boned and fine featured. Even allowing for the fact that the sculptor would be trying to flatter, they do have an unearthly kind of beauty.

18

There is little to see of Astley Castle now, except ruined walls and empty window sockets like sightless eyes. But as with every ruin, there is an air of romance, and as with every ruin there are ghosts. Local legend has it that the headless spectre of Suffolk has been seen flitting hither and thither. He cannot find his oak tree because it was blown down in a gale in 1891. There is also the soft gliding apparition of a black monk, lingering between church and castle.

Strangely, there are no ghosts of Astley's two sad Queens. Neither Elizabeth Woodville mourning for her two little boys, the princes in the Tower, nor gentle Jane the Nine Days Queen, both pawns in the bloody political game of their age, return to haunt the ruin which was once their home and where both of them in their turn knew happiness.

Atherstone

Atherstone, in north Warwickshire, stands upon the old Roman road of Watling Street, and has a well preserved milestone which is either inaccurate or has been moved around from time to time, for it declares it to be 200 miles to London.

Nowadays, traffic can bypass Atherstone and this has left its main road, Long Street (upon the old Watling Street), comparatively quiet and peaceful. Except, of course, every Shrove Tuesday, when a most unusual football match takes place.

It is believed that the game of football was actually 'invented' in Atherstone, for the game has been played here, up and down Long Street, almost since the time of King John. It is a somewhat hectic and erratic game, which used to go on most of the day, but is now more or less confined to a couple of hours. The main protagonists were the Warwickshire Lads versus the Leicestershire Lads from over the border, and the prize was a bag of gold. The original ball was a pig's or beast's bladder.

Things have changed a bit since the days of King John! Teams are now from factions within the town, and the game is usually set off by a well-known personality who throws the ball from

19

the window of the Blue Bell Inn, in the famous Long Street. The shop windows up and down the street are boarded up for the occasion, and afterwards, no matter which side is the winner, there is a collection for some worthy local charity. Many people attend this event, and a good time is had by all.

Atherstone's Long Street is one of the finest in the county, with a variety of architectural styles and lovely old coaching inns. Long Street was on the regular coaching route, and Atherstone and its inns catered extensively for passengers.

Another thing which made Atherstone famous all over the world was the hatting industry. Why they started to make felt hats at Atherstone has never been made clear, but certainly they were doing it in Tudor times, and in the 18th century entrepreneurs moved in and turned what was a very small scale cottage industry into a profitable commercial enterprise.

One of the things that caused the eventual disintegration of the felt hat industry was, strangely enough, the abolition of the slave trade. British colonial slave owners were compelled by law to provide felt hats for their slaves. One of those odd quirks, for no law compelled them to feed them properly, or provide medical attention, but it did insist upon felt hats. Most of these hats were made in Atherstone. Consequently no slaves, no hats, no work! As a result of this, the 1820s saw vast unemployment in Atherstone. So great was the hardship that the owner of nearby Merevale Hall, Dugdale Stratford Dugdale, descendant of the same Sir William Dugdale who wrote *Antiquities of Warwickshire* plus many other volumes, commissioned unemployed men to build a high wall all around his estate. They were paid in food, and the wall took several years to build. When it was completed, the men clubbed together and presented Mr Dugdale with a silver cup to show their gratitude.

Not far from Atherstone is Bosworth field, and it was here in this town in 1485 that Henry Tudor, later to become King Henry VII, met Lord Stanley at Halls Close and persuaded him to transfer his allegiance from Richard III to the Tudors. Stanley, ever on the winning side, didn't need much persuasion, and it was largely because he switched allegiance, on the night before

Bosworth, that Richard III lost his crown. Henry Tudor took communion in Atherstone's parish church of St Mary before riding off to fight.

Another more peaceful name, and a name to be reckoned with, is connected with St Mary's, Atherstone. Obadiah Grew ran his small grammar school inside the church here. He was a dedicated Puritan in his beliefs, and yet he personally pleaded with Oliver Cromwell to spare the life of his King, Charles I. He was flung into gaol in his old age, and went blind, but remained undaunted, dictating his sermons to friends who visited him. These were then copied and sent to all those churches around about, where Grew was held in esteem and affection.

Obadiah Grew had a son, who became more famous than his father. Nehemiah Grew was born in Atherstone in 1628, and from childhood shared his father's love of plants and growing things. He is now often referred to as the 'father of English botany' and he was the author of the pioneering *Anatomy of Plants* and, as he was a physician, *The Comparative Anatomy of the Stomach and Guts* (1681). He was the Secretary of the Royal Society from 1677.

Atherstone has a long, long history, stretching from Roman times, for upon the remains of Watling Street, marks of chariot wheels were discovered many years ago. It wears its age well, and now that a bypass removes all through traffic Atherstone can once more feel itself 'hidden', except for those who choose to go and find it.

Baddesley Ensor

▬ Baddesly Ensor is a mining village in the north of the county, rambling close by the old Roman road of Watling Street. Here in the year 1869 there occurred a dreadful murder, callous and brutal, with no apparent motive, that shook the small close-knit community to its very core.

The victim was 22 year old Harriet Atkins; a pretty, lively local girl, wife of miner Michael Atkins, and mother of his two year old child. Harriet was once more heavily pregnant, and was expecting to be confined at any hour. Her second child was to be a Christmas baby. Alas, the poor little mite never saw the light of day.

Harriet Atkins was the daughter of the local butcher at Baddesley Ensor, and her parents lived only a few doors up the street from the Atkins home. She was a loving and dutiful daughter, and regularly popped in to see her parents who were devoted to her. They had been disappointed when their pretty daughter married Michael Atkins. They didn't like the young man, although Harriet had fallen readily enough for his rough good looks and light hearted nature. He had the reputation of being a ne'er do well; he was irresponsible, and spent far too much time showing off to his mates in the pubs, declared Harriet's parents. They wanted better for their daughter, but Harriet got her own way and the couple were married.

The marriage was not a success. Michael Atkins spent all his money on drink, declaring it was his because he had earned it by working down the mine. Harriet and her child were left short of essentials, and her parents frequently came to her aid with gifts of food and money. For Harriet her parents would do anything to help, but they refused to allow Michael Atkins across their threshold. They could not forgive his brutality towards their beloved daughter, who regularly appeared with black eyes and bruises, caused when Michael knocked her about after an evening at the local pub with his friends.

It is probable that the parents confided their worries to the local vicar, for he began to take an interest in Harriet and Michael. He gave Michael a few good talkings-to, and discovered the young man had a pleasant singing voice. This led the vicar, musical himself, to persuade Michael Atkins to join his singing classes. For a while he attended the singing classes without fail and stopped going to the pub. The home life of Harriet and Michael improve enormously, but it didn't last. Michael Atkins soon got bored, and it wasn't long before he was once more a regular down at the pub, the Mount Pleasant.

This was the state of affairs on 11th December 1869. Atkins told his wife he was going to the vicarage to the singing class, and accordingly made himself tidy before setting off. But he didn't go near the vicarage. He went to the Mount Pleasant instead, where it was noticed he drank heavily and was in a defiant mood.

He left about ten o'clock with a man named Day, who lived in the same road as himself. They neared the Atkins house, and then stood chatting for a minute or two. They saw another neighbour, a man called Jim Bedford, with whom they exchanged greetings.

The conversation exhausted, Atkins said 'Goodnight' and went into his own house. Before either of the men, Day and Bedford, could move off, they heard the sound of a gunshot. Startled, they stopped in their tracks, and then Atkins came running out of his house shouting 'Harriet has shot herself!'

Bedford and Day ran with all speed into the house, and were there confronted with the horrific sight of Harriet Atkins lying in bed in a pool of her own blood. At the inquest held later, the evidence was that the muzzle of a gun had been held no more than twelve inches from the dead woman's face when the trigger was squeezed, since some of the wadding used to pack the powder and ball was found within her dreadful wounds. Harriet Atkins had died instantly.

Day fetched Harriet's parents, and her father, seeing his dead and dearly loved daughter, turned on Michael Atkins crying 'You rogue. You have killed her'. He would have attacked Atkins had he not been restrained.

The inquest brought a verdict of wilful murder against Michael Atkins, who appeared at Warwick Assizes to answer to the charge. The evidence given in court by both Day and Bedford was perfectly clear. They heard a scream, then a gunshot. Atkins had then run into the street declaring his wife had shot herself. When they entered the room, they saw the poor woman lying dead, killed instantly according to medical evidence, and the death weapon a shotgun. Michael Atkins had a shotgun. It was kept on the wall above the fireplace, hanging firmly upon two nails. Yet when Bedford and Day went into the room, the shotgun was in its accustomed place, upon the two nails. It was the gun that killed Harriet.

If Harriet had died instantly, how could she possibly have

got out of bed to hang the shotgun back upon its nails, and returned to bed to die? With her, of course, died the babe she was carrying.

Atkins maintained an appearance of stolid and total indifference during the whole time he was in gaol and when he appeared before the court. No flicker of emotion crossed his young and good looking face. And yet, when he saw the judge don the black cap and pronounce the death sentence, he fainted in the dock.

Barcheston

This has to be one of Warwickshire's tiniest villages, for it contains nothing but three houses and a church. Its approach is via winding lanes and were it not for the church tower no one would really know it exists.

But it was not always so. It is one of the county's most famous depopulated villages, and the villain of the piece lies recumbent within the church of St Martin, in a superb alabaster tomb whereon his effigy reposes, with his wife, Ann, by his side. William Willington purchased Barcheston in 1507, and promptly set about enclosure, turning peasants off their land, and putting sheep upon it. He thus became very rich, and with some of his gains built the Willington Chapel within the church. William Willington and Ann had seven daughters, all of whom married into the most notable families in the shire.

One of them, Mary, married William Sheldon, and upon Willington's death in 1555, the Sheldons acquired Barcheston. William sent his son Ralph, together with Richard Hyckes of Barcheston, on the Grand Tour of Europe with instructions to learn about weaving tapestries. Upon their return looms were set up in the manor house at Barcheston, and for the next century the Barcheston tapestries became famous. There are examples to be seen in the Victoria & Albert museum, and the famous tapestry map of Warwickshire was purchased some years ago and presented to Warwickshire County Museum by the Courtauld Institute. It covers one wall of the upper room in the Market Place Museum, Warwick.

The church of St Martin was built upon the site of a much earlier St Augustine church, of which there were but six in the area during the 7th century. St Martin's was built 1270-1280, and dedicated to St Martin of Tours in 1291. The font is said to have been a gift from King Edward I and Queen Eleanor, and two of the heads with which it is ornamented are supposed to be likenesses of the Royal couple.

It is the tower of St Martin's that attracts attention, for it can be seen for several miles in many directions. And it leans! Very noticeably, does it lean! It is 56ft high, with walls ten feet thick. It has no proper foundation, and leans a full 20 inches to the west. The tower was rebuilt in the time of Queen Elizabeth I and two priest's chambers, one with a fireplace, were built into it, together with stone seats shaped like armchairs. It is likely that Hugh Humphrey, priest of Barcheston in the early 16th century, lived here.

There was something of a sensation early one morning in the year 1635 when the few inhabitants left in Barcheston awoke to find thieves had been busy in the night and stripped all the lead from the church roof. The churchwardens recorded they 'went to surch' for the missing lead. They were subsequently required to travel to Worcester where Richard Trafford, a tinker, and John Mumford, glazier, were suspected of stealing the lead. There is, however, no record of these two men coming to trial.

The churchwardens' accounts then list all the expenses involved in getting lead back on the roof. It cost them £2 16s to cast eight and twenty hundred of lead at two shillings the hundred! Then they had to fetch the 'soder', fetch and carry the sand, hire a mason, buy the nails, and fell a few trees to provide fuel to facilitate the melting of the lead. Altogether a long and expensive piece of work.

There used at one time to be three chained books within the church; the *Treatise of Erasmus* (1548), *Common Places of Christian Religion* (1587) and *Sermon of John Jewel* (1611). But alas, things being what they now are, it was considered these should be deposited with the County Record Office for safety.

Domed memorial fountain at Barton on the Heath

Barton-on-the-Heath

One of Warwickshire's most idyllic villages, with nothing to mar its tranquillity or detract from its aged beauty. And yet it is not one of those self-consciously 'pretty' villages; it is not seen on postcards, or the lids of biscuit tins. It just appears to have evolved in a way that is both comfortable and pleasing.

It clusters around a large village green, in the centre of which is an elaborate domed memorial fountain of 1874. There are trees, mellow stone houses and cottages, and views across the vale of Moreton that are quite unsurpassed.

Barton-on-the-Heath has Shakespearian connections, as indeed do most Warwickshire villages. Here lived Edmund Lambert, who married Shakespeare's Aunt Joan, sister to his mother, Mary Arden. When William's father, John, was in some financial difficulties, he borrowed money on surety from Edmund Lambert and although he eventually achieved the wherewithal to pay off his debt, it took until the next generation to resolve the matter.

Shakespeare must have visited his Lambert cousins at Barton-on-the-Heath many times, and would have been familiar with the houses, fields and woodlands of this village. He used it in *The Taming of the Shrew* when he has the tinker say, 'Am I not Christopher Sly, old Sly's son of Burtonheath, by birth a pedlar, by education a cardmaker, by transmutation a bear-herd, and now by present profession a tinker ...?'

Here too lived Dr James Wilmot, ironically the very man who first declared that Francis Bacon wrote the famous plays and not William Shakespeare at all. Dr Wilmot is described as a tall imposing figure with flowing hair, a concave face and a self satisfied expression (*Gentleman's Magazine* 1813). He was a Senior Fellow of Trinity College, Oxford, and son of Thomas Wilmot, an inn keeper at Warwick.

Wilmot took up the living at Barton-on-the-Heath in 1782, occupying the rectory with his ten year old niece Olive, supposedly the daughter of his brother 'Black Bob' Wilmot, so called because he made off with some of the rates after being made treasurer of Warwick. It later transpired there was some doubt about James Wilmot's so called niece; that she was in fact his own grand daughter, child of his daughter Olive, who as a young woman was secretly married to the Duke of Cumberland. Her descendants subsequently brought a court case in an attempt to get 'Princess Olive' recognised by the Crown, but in this they were unsuccessful.

James Wilmot began to study Sheakespeare while at Oxford, and he eventually came to his extraordinary conclusion that the true author was Francis Bacon. His theory met with little credence in his lifetime, but there is now a Francis Bacon Society, founded in the 1930s, who still regard James Wilmot as their true founder, and afford him appropriate honour.

This was not all the good doctor got up to! He was suspected of being the author of the Junius letters. These 70 satirical epistles on public affairs first appeared in the *Public Advertiser* between 1769 and 1772, and were subsequently printed in bookform. They were frankly critical, some even say scurrilous, and have been described as the forerunner of the present day 'leading article'. Their author was sought for, at some length, but was never found. The finger pointed towards Dr Wilmot, but indeed if he it was, and the idea was well within keeping with his character, then he kept silent about it.

The tempestuous Olive and the blustering Dr Wilmot must have made quite a stir in the quiet backwater of Barton-on-the-Heath. Wilmot went blind towards the end of his life, and died at Barton in 1807.

He is buried in the chancel of St Lawrence's church at Barton-on-the-Heath, and his memorial tablet is very close to the chancel arch. And upon the chancel arch is a very strange thing. Carved upon one side is an extraordinary stylised animal, just one, all on its own, and no amount of looking can determine its exact species. It has long ears, a snout and a tail, yet one would scarce dare to declare it a pig. No one seems to know who put it there or why, but perhaps it was a humorous quirk on the part of one of the masons who built this church some eight centuries ago. Perhaps he did it as a joke, and made his fellow craftsmen laugh!

In front of the alter is a brass to Edmund Bury and his wife, Elizabeth Underhill. Edmund Bury died in 1588, and Elizabeth married again, a Thomas Sawyer of Northampton, where she went to live. Thomas Sawyer died and Elizabeth, homesick, wanted to return to her native heath, so she instructed she should be buried in the chancel at Barton-on-the-Heath, with the body of her first husband. Poor Tom Sawyer was left alone, it seems.

Another memorial tablet, quaintly worded, emphasises the impact the enclosures must have had on this area, the fringes of the Cotswolds, from whence came the sheep known as Cotswold Lions and upon whose back was founded the great prosperity of the wool trade. Many landowners deliberately forced peasants off their strips of land, and pulled down their hovels in order to breed sheep upon these wide acres. Upon William Sands's memorial, we are told he was born in this parish in December 1720 'Being the Hundredth Year After the Enclosure'. He was of the Honourable Band of Gentlemen Pensioners in the reign of George III for 40 years, and 'having lived to a good old age in general good health and good fortune, finished with good hope on May 15the 1802...'.

Next door to the church is the manor house, known as Barton House, where one assumes Edmund Bury and Elizabeth Underhill once lived. It was built upon the site of a much older house and is attributed to Inigo Jones although there is some controversy about it. However, if it wasn't Inigo Jones himself then it must have been someone who studies his work, for whoever the architect was, he has come up with something that looks absolutely just right and in which every aspect pleases.

Bascote Heath

➤ Bascote Heath is very much a hidden part of Warwickshire. It is on the old drovers' road still called Welsh Road, coming form Wales and heading towards London. Bascote lives not far from the town of Southam, which Charles I so disliked. It seems this stemmed from the fact that when he went into Southam in 1641, before hostilities properly started, the townsfolk were so completely indifferent to his Royal presence that nobody bothered to ring the bell of the 126 ft high steeple in their parish church.

The Kings' men took exception to this omission, and went into the church, locking the doors behind them, so that the townsfolk were denied entry. Only the payment of quite a large sum of money persuaded them to reopen the doors, and this payment is recorded in the churchwardens' accounts.

However, presumably the King decided to let bygones be bygones, for the following year he again visited Southam and stayed the night within the town. He was on his way to Nottingham to raise the Standard. On his way thither, he passed through Bascote Heath. Even now, in the 20th century, Bascote Heath is deserted; what it must have been like in the 17th century is difficult to envisage. However, the King's forces were ambushed by Parliamentarian troopers upon the heath, and there was a lively skirmish. How lively is not recorded, except that 50 of the King's men were killed or injured and he lost quite a few pieces of artillery. However, the Royalists made their getaway, and raised the Standard at Nottingham on 25th August 1642.

There is a handful of houses at Bascote, no more than that. At Bascote Heath, deep within the woodlands which line the road, and where once the butterfly orchids used to bloom, is a tiny cemetery, approached by leaning rustic wooden gates, with a pithy notice which says 'Passers by, Gipsy and Gentry alike, are requested to leave no litter'. It seems to have worked, I'm glad to say.

It is an extraordinary graveyard, deeply hidden, and with no notice to indicate that it is there or to whom it belongs. There is no church nearer than Southam, which has its own large graveyard, and one cannot help but wonder why this one was made minus church or chapel, in such an isolated spot. Why should these 40 or so people choose to be buried here, unless for the very simple reason that it is so quiet, secluded and beautiful.

There are some very interesting headstones, notably those to the Chamberlayne family of Stoneythorpe, a tiny parish not far away which has now become a part of Southam, to all intents and purposes. The grand house of the Chamberlayne now serves as an hotel, but the family lived there for many years.

The Chamberlayne graves are in a row at Bascote Heath, but two of them are unusual. Mrs Evelyn Chamberlayne, 'wife of W. T. Chamberlayne', died in January 1931, just two months before her son, William Francis Chamberlayne. Their headstones stand side by side, with the plain commonplace details on the face. Upon the back of the headstones, though, their are lines of poetry. Upon that of Mrs Evelyn Chamberlayne, is carved the whole 16 lines of Tennyson's *Crossing the Bar* which begins:

> Sunset and evening star
> And one clear call for me
> And may there be no moaning of the bar
> When I put out to sea.

Her son has 14 lines beginning 'Careless seems the Great Avenger...'.

The last Chamberlayne appears to be Commander Tankerville Chamberlayne, RN, who was born in Argentina in 1900 and died in Jersey where he was buried in 1971. There is a rather grand memorial tablet to his memory, describing him as 'remembered with love'.

Billesley

Billesley is a tiny Arcadia, set amid green fields and winding lanes only a few miles west of Stratford. It is on the site of a much earlier settlement known as Billesley Trussell, completely wiped out by the Black Death.

There exists the old manor house, now a prestigious hotel, and a handful of nearby houses. In the grounds of the old manor is the tiny church around which much controversy has recently raged. The church of All Saints is now defunct, and was built in 1692 upon the site of a much older church. It is thought that this might be where Shakespeare was married, and a recent exploration in the crypt below the sealed church has led one man to believe there are papers and records down there which might throw light upon the subject. To date, however, further exploration has been refused. It is known that in this church, some 30 years after the poet's death, his only surviving descendant, his grand-daughter Elizabeth Nash, a widow, married her second husband, John Barnard.

In this church too a quaint custom prevailed during the last century when a Mr Knottesford, who lived at Alveston, ministered until his death in 1859. He was a grand old man, a man of strong principle, who refused to give his servants any work to don on the Sabbath. Every Sunday, he and his family and their servants all piled into coaches at Alveston and drove the six miles to Billesley, where they had morning service at 11 o'clock. After service, lunch was served in the pews, the footman spreading a white cloth and a cold collation prepared the day before, over the seats. After lunch, while the elders dozed, the servants and the children played in the churchyard and grounds, until three o'clock in the afternoon when it was once more time for divine service. After this, the entire party drove the six miles home again.

The Trussell family lived at Billesley for generations. Richard Trussell was killed at the Battle of Evesham fighting with Simon de Montfort on the side of the great barons, and because of this his estate was seized by the Crown. His brother William eventually got it back again, and he it was who served as Speaker in the Parliament which denounced King Edward II. In 1501 Shakespeare's maternal grandfather Robert Arden agreed to act as trustee for some of the Trussell property but in 1588 Thomas Trussell, the last of the family, was hanged for highway robbery and once again Billesley passed to the Crown. In 1592 it was bought by Robert Lee, Lord Mayor of London, who together with his son Sir Robert Lee largely rebuilt the old house, and had its timber framing clad with stone from quarries at Wilmcote close by.

Shakespeare knew Billesley very well. It is believed that he was given free run of the extensive library of the Lee family and actually wrote most of *As Your Like It* there. After his death, when his home New Place was rebuilt by the Cloptons, some of the panelling was removed to line the library at Billesley.

The manor passed through many hands. In 1912 Henry Burton Tate, son of the founder of the Tate Gallery, lived here for 20 years or so. One of his guests, during the period between the wars, was Bruce Bairnsfather, the cartoonist of the First World War and creator of the character 'Old Bill'.

Binton

Binton, with its adjoining hamlet of Lower Binton, is grouped around the lower slopes of Binton Hill, a few miles west of Stratford-upon-Avon. It was on open and desolate land near here that the meetings of the court of the old 'Barlichway' Hundred met centuries ago, and a nearby farm with the name Barley Leys, a corruption of 'Barlichway', commemorates the fact.

There is little at Lower Binton except farms and fields stretching out towards the Warwickshire plain, but as the road winds flat and gentle towards Binton it arrives at a crossroads, still leafy and well wooded, with an old stone well on one corner, the church of St Peter on rising ground on the other, and the old rectory just below it. The church is not especially interesting, since it was only built in 1875, replacing an older church on the same site. However, it does have one great treasure. The Scott window, unveiled in 1915, and paid for by public subscription.

Captain Robert Falcon Scott, the leader of the ill-fated Antarctic expedition of 1910, spent his last few days in England right here in Binton. His wife, Kathleen, was the sister of Rev Hervey Bruce, the last resident rector of this place. The Scotts often visited the rectory, and this time they came to say farewell before Captain Scott set off on the *Terra Nova* with Dr Wilson, Oates, Bowers and Evans. In that year of 1910, Binton was a picture book village full of old timbered cottages and thatch, of narrow unmade roads and leafy ways. This was the last glimpse of the English countryside for the brave Captain Scott.

The west window in the church of St Peter tells the whole

story. In quiet colour we see first Captain Scott and his colleagues, happy and confident, on their way south to plant the British flag. Then we see their bitter disappointment when after a fearsome march of 69 days and great privation, they realise that Amundsen had beaten them to it, and the Norwegian flag flew at the Pole. We see the tragic and gallant scene as Captain Oates walked out into the raging blizzard in an attempt to save the lives of his companions; and the final scene some eight months later when the bodies of these brave men were discovered still inside their tent by the search party, who erected a stone cairn to mark their last resting place.

Below the window hangs a photograph of Captain Scott and another of the whole group, Oates, Little Bowers, Dr Wilson and Petty Officer Evans, taken amid the icy wastes on 18th January 1911. It seems that Bowers set the camera up, posed everyone, and then rushed to sit down in the group himself. They all look so hopeful and confident.

The story of the Scott expedition has stirred the imagination for so many years; the desperate plight of this brave group, and their ultimate death in isolation and loneliness. It is strange to think that such a national event, such national heroes, should be thus remembered in this small Warwickshire village, that the Scotts held in great affection.

Immediately below the west window is the Roll of Honour for those who fell in the First World War, and the first name upon the list is that of the rector's son, Captain Scott's nephew.

Birdingbury

This pleasant village, somewhat to the east of the Roman Fosse Way, is on the river Leam. There are some nice old cottages, along rather narrow lanes, and quite a lot of new housing has spread the village out from its original centre.

What does catch the eye is the church, for it is a most unusual edifice to find in a very small Warwickshire village. Architectural experts have described it variously as 'classical' which it certainly is, or 'a putty coloured Doric temple' with Victorian Gothick windows. It lies well back, surrounded by a large churchyard. It is austere and rather cold. Doubtless it replaced a much more homely building.

34

St Leonard's was altered in 1873, but almost certainly it was built in the time of Birdingbury's most famous rector, Rev Henry Homer, who lived here, in the rectory, from 1764 until his death in 1791. Henry Homer was a man whose ideas were far in advance of his age, and he held strong views upon most things, notably those that had a dire effect upon the rural community in which he lived and worked.

He wrote prolifically about the Enclosure Acts which were then causing both distress and concern. He wrote about the plight of the poor; about the state of the roads and how important was their preservation and improvement. He wrote of the open field system, and of navigation. In an age when clergymen were supposed to concentrate upon their calling, and were considered by and large to be a part of the establishment, of the recognised order of things, Henry Homer was on the side of those who stood to lose most.

He had 17 children, all of whom dutifully accompanied him to his church every Sabbath. he sent seven of his sons to Rugby, and his tenth son, Philip Bracebridge Homer, classical scholar and poet, became a master at that school. where he remained until his death in 1838. Arthur, the fourth son, became rector of Standlake. He too was a classical scholar, friend of the famous. He wrote *Bibliographica Americana* and died in 1806.

Henry Homer (the younger) too was a classical scholar and assisted in the publication of *Bellenden's Tracts* in 1787. He died just a few months before his father, and they are buried together in the churchyard at Birdingbury. It seems strange that such as family should have no memorial within the church they served so well. Presumably in the heavy restoration of 1873, any traces of the Homers were removed.

Bowshot Crossroads

The Romans came to Warwickshire, and indeed they could hardly have helped it, since being right in the middle of the country they must have had to march through it no matter where they were headed.

The left us two important roads; the Fosse Way which cuts right across the country, and Watling Street which skirts the north-eastern boundary. There is a third, Icknield Street, which cuts across the Alcester area to the north-west, but this merely pops in and out of the county, rather than crossing it.

Many experts have decided that although Watling Street and the Fosse Way are, in effect, Roman roads, it is likely they were there long before these stalwart and civilised people invaded us. They were well-used and well-worn tracks made by ancient man who, being possessed of more commonsense than most of us give him credit for, simply walked in a straight line to wherever he was going. The Romans must have looked at those straight tracks and decided to make them more sophisticated, more serviceable, and their engineers got to work. Very good work too, since the roads still serve us.

The Fosse Way is pleasant, and for much of its Warwickshire length goes through some particularly beautiful countryside. The area where it crosses the main road between Kineton and Wellesbourne has acquired the name 'Bowshot' crossroads, and thereby hangs a tale! The motorist busy hurtling onwards towards Leicester may negotiate this crossroads without a passing glance. For years, the County Council have busily 'improved' it, and there are now so many black and white striped notices that any tale of romance of yesteryear is long forgotten.

In the days of Henry II (1133-1189) this road formed the boundary between two large estates, Compton Murdac (now called Compton Verney) and Walton. Roger Murdac owned Compton, and William D'Eivile owned Walton which, naturally enough, was called after him, Walton D'Eivile. The two men were friends as well as neighbours, and enjoyed nothing so much as a day's sport. They both owned greyhounds, and there was considerable rivalry between them.

One day, being fair and fine, they met by chance and decided to settle once and for all the perpetually vexing question of who owned the best greyhound. A contest was rapidly organised, with a rough track marked out. The prize was to be land! The winner was to take as much land from the loser's estate as could be covered by a bowshot, in length and breadth.

The race was won by Murdac's dog, and thus the land at Bowshot came to the Compton estate. Murdac did, however, agree to give D'Eivile a bag of pepper (a kind of 'peppercorn rent') on the following Easter day. The name still lingers not only in the busy crossroads, but also in the abutting woodland, yet the origins of it do not appear to arouse much curiosity.

There are many tales of ghosts along the Fosse Way. One part of it towards the north of the county is said to be haunted by a Roman legion, which still marches. Where it is going, we know not, but this ghostly hundred has been seen upon more than one occasion. The only difficulty is that they appear to have been cut off at the knees! Then it was realised that the original surface of this ancient road must have been at least a foot lower than it is at present, so with leather clad feet, the hundred march silently on the original surface of the road, their feet and ankles totally invisible.

Brailes

Although the village as a whole could never be said to be hidden in any sense of the word, one small part of it is! It was well hidden through all the troublesome times of religious persecution, and its isolation and what might be called almost 'disguise' allowed its survival. Now, although it no longer strives to hide, few people could find it out unless they knew well where to look.

Down a tiny lane called Friars Lane, across a piece of open land, and up a tiny path lies Rectory Farm. A covered flight of stones steps alongside the old timbered house leads into what was once an old malt barn and later converted to a Catholic chapel, one of the earliest in the Midlands.

Before the Dissolution of the Monasteries, Rectory Farm was a part of the friars' living, and when it was sold, the Bishop family bought it. Here was born William Bishop in 1554.

The Guild of Our Lady had supported two priests and a tiny grammar school in Friars Lane, but this too was ended in 1548. Again, the Bishops managed to buy some of the land, and endowed the continuation of the little school. Later they lent financial support to a Catholic one, which had perforce to be of a secret nature. John Bishop, father of William, is buried in the parish church of St George, with a fine monumental inscription telling us he died on the 'third day of April 1601'.

William was educated in Brailes, and then went to Oxford. When he came back home in 1574, he gave up his share of the not inconsiderable Bishop estate to his brother and went abroad to Douai, then Rheims and Rome, becoming ordained in 1583. When he returned to this country with the English mission he was promptly arrested and taken before Sir Francis Walsingham, Elizabeth's Secretary of State, before being flung into the Marshalsea, to suffer the horrors for which that place has become notorious. Upon his release he returned to Paris.

William Bishop worked tirelessly for the Catholic cause, but more than this he worked for a greater understanding, and accordingly seemed to become involved in much controversy. He was imprisoned for a second time in 1611, for refusing to take the oath of Allegiance demanded by James I, but again he was released shortly after.

On 4th June 1623, he was consecrated Bishop of Chalcedon in Paris. He landed at Dover on 31st July, and despite his 70 years he walked the 13 miles to Eltham, where he was warmly received. Once again, he was in the thick of the struggle, and worked among the faithful. The work took its toll, and less than a year later, in April 1624, he died and was buried at Old Pancras.

Although he is the most famous of the Bishop family, there was yet another whose life was forfeit. Elizabeth, daughter of Francis, decided to become a nun at the age of 17, and in September 1707 she left her home in Brailes to enter a convent abroad accompanied by two friends, Winifred Elliot and Elizabeth Hilliard. Two other girls seeking education, Anne Scandrele and Catherine Jeffs, were of the same party.

Upon arriving at Ostend, the girls were importuned by a soldier who had been a prison of war in France, had broken his parole, and was on his way back home. He received short shrift for his unwelcome overtures, and thinking himself no end of a fellow, he did not take kindly to the rebuff. He decided to take revenge upon the girls by reporting them to the mayor of Ostend as being guilty of treason by leaving England and entering a foreign country without permission. On 23rd September, they were taken into custody in Ostend.

On 8th December, they were put on board an English vessel which was to take them home, but in a very short space of time the ship was driven back by stormy seas and dashed to pieces against the pier. Elizabeth and her companions, together with others, were flung overboard and their bodies were crushed against the piles of the pier. When they were recovered, they were bruised and broken almost beyond recognition. The girls were buried together in a common grave, and their funeral procession was headed by 30 virgins. In the funeral address, they were called 'Martyrs for their faith and conquerors of impiety...'.

Elizabeth's brother, George, also went to Douai for his studies and was ordained in Paris in 1717. He returned to his native hearth, Brailes, to serve and he was instrumental in converting the old malt barn into a Catholic chapel, which he courageously opened to the public in 1726. Courageously, because the laws prohibiting the celebration of the Catholic mass were not repealed until 1778, and there was still a great deal of religious persecution.

But Rev George obviously felt it necessary to allow the faithful to come into the little secret chapel for worship, and in this he was fully supported by his brother Richard. It still has many of its original features, including the lovely polished sloping floors and the fine panelling. George Bishop was also responsible for the publication in 1752 of the *Poor Man's Catechism*.

The Bishop family served their church well, and there are many memorials in the churchyard bearing their names. After the Dissolution, they stuck fast to the Old Faith, and indeed must have hidden many priests in the various 'hides' in Rectory Farm.

The Bishop estate was finally sold in 1911, when the chapel and its contents passed into the care of the Archdiocese of

Birmingham. It is still approached by the uneven stone staircase on the outside of the farmhouse, these steps echoing to the tread of the faithful every Sunday.

Burton Dassett

The way to Burton Dassett is winding, for this depopulated village is perfectly hidden, tucked away in the folds of the Dassett Hills. The very name Dassett is taken from the Saxon Dercetone, meaning the abode of wild beasts, and those with a little imagination will have no difficulty in visualising what it was like here so many centuries ago, before the Conquest.

Burton Dassett was a thriving community in medieval times but little remains of its prosperity, although its beauty, seclusion and tranquillity continue. It now consists of a farm, and one of the finest churches in the country, with a holy well outside its gates. Above the well, where water still gurgles, is a well house with Grecian-style pillars. Some references date the well from 1534, with the Grecian part of the well house added for decoration round about 1840. Inside, in the green gloom, ferns grow from its walls and roof.

The Saxons lived here, for in 1908 a Saxon burial place was discovered on the hill called Mount Pleasant. In two trenches were 35 skeletons, with pottery and weapons. From the injuries it would appear they were killed in battle sometime in the 7th century.

In the 13th century this place was so prosperous that Henry III granted it a market every Friday, and it was known as Chipping Dassett. Then came the Black Death, rampaging throughout the land and severely decimating the population. Burton Dassett did not properly recover, and the actions of a wicked landlord completed its depopulation. Burton Dassett belonged to Ralph Boteler, who owned a great deal of Warwickshire. He was Standard Bearer to Henry VI and was created Baron Sudeley. But he was childless and upon his death the property was divided between his two sisters, one of whom was married into the Belknap family. The Belknaps owned the manor for three generations, and dealt fairly; then came Sire Edward Belknap, with no other thought in his head except that of making money.

He did not live at Burton Dassett but at Weston-under-Weatherly, just a few miles off. When he acquired Burton Dassett at the end of the 15th century, it took him no time at all to realise that the hills which enfolded it were ideal for sheep rearing. The wool market was a prosperous one, and wool staplers were getting rich very quickly. Sir Edward evicted 60 people and pulled down their houses to enclose 600 acres for his sheep. It was at that time illegal to pull down any houses used for agricultural purposes, but this didn't bother Sir Edward one whit. He had great influence at Court, for he was one of Henry VII's commanders at the Battle of Stoke, a Commissioner of Array for Warwickshire, a Commander at the Battle of Blackheath, Keeper of Warwick Castle, and Squire of the Body to the King himself. He avoided having to pay the fines levied

The Beacon at Burton Dassett

upon such acts of wanton destruction by spending money on the church thus, he declared, making it a better place *because* of his sheep rearing project.

He also built a beacon tower, and added this to his coat of arms. The beacon still exists, and it was on the top of this edifice that a great fire was flaming to spread the news across the country of the Battle of Edgehill, fought within sight of these hills on 23rd October 1642. Legend also has it that an up-and-coming captain by the name of Oliver Cromwell, then aged 43, climbed up this tower to see what was happening in all the confusion of the battle. Learning a valuable military lesson, he went off and formed his Ironsides, whose discipline was a byword.

The hills enclosed by the wicked Sir Edward are now open again, and were acquired by Warwickshire County Council some years ago for use as a country park.

One visitor to Burton Dassett did not meet with a very warm welcome, and made his feelings known. It was during the Wars of the Roses that a ragged, barefoot orphan boy came stumbling through the winter lanes to Burton Dassett begging bread. The people did not take kindly to beggars and so they turned the boy away, cold and hungry.

He stumbled on to the nearby hamlets of Northend and Knightcote, where he was given bread, such as they had, and a place by the fires so that he could get warm. The following morning, the urchin thanked his kind hosts, and once more set off on foot. He got as far as Mollington, just over the Oxfordshire border, where he got work, and eventually became a prosperous farmer in his own right. But he never forgot those who helped him at a time when he needed it most.

He died in 1469, and the people of Northend and Knightcote were astonished to learn he had left them dole bread money. The people of Burton Dassett were to receive nothing, but he did leave seven shillings a year to be spent on the upkeep of their church. To this day the charity exists, and benefits every Christmas the people of the two parishes who were kindly disposed to share with a ragged urchin the little they had. Over the years, the trustees of John Kimble's Charity have faithfully doled out help to the needy. A cottage in Knightcote was bought and turned into a school, with the schoolmaster paid from John Kimble's Charity, and money has been spent on the church. Nowadays, the money is given in various ways to those who need help, and the children of Northend and Knightcote receive a gift every Christmas. Truly a case of 'casting your bread upon the waters' and John Kimble is remembered on a stone tablet within the church of All Saints at Burton Dassett, for all time.

Chesterton

Little remains of this village now, except a handful of scattered houses, mostly modern, just north of what was once a Roman camp. This is a backwater, and has enjoyed the seclusion this status carries for a century or so. Now, sadly, the peace is likely to be eroded with the new M40 motorway passing close by, plainly visible and audible from the hills.

The village was described by Pevsner in his *Buildings of England* (1966) as 'an eerie place which lost its heart when it lost the grand and curious mansion of the Peytos'. But the great Inigo Jones was a friend of Sir Edward Peyto, and Chesterton, depopulated village though it may be, has more than its fair share of treasured examples of the work of this talented man.

The 'curious' mansion mentioned by Pevsner was built around 1635/40 and was described as a 'rustic version' of the Banqueting House in Whitehall, also by Inigo Jones.

Sir Edward Peyto was learned and erudite man. He it was who defended Warwick Castle in the Civil War and, when challenged by the enemy, ran up a Bible as his flag, declaring himself to be faithful unto God. He was an astrologer and mathematician, and was greatly interested in architecture, hence his friendship with Jones.

Sir Edward, not content merely with his curious mansion, also had his friend design for him an arch so that the Peyto family could walk across the field and enter the little church of St Giles through a private doorway. This doorway is now walled up but the arch remains, and is shortly to be restored and repaired. It looks lost, standing as it does on the extreme edge

Sir Edward Peyto's windmill, Chesterton

of the churchyard, looking down on to what in medieval times was called the tournament field, and thence across the small valley to all that remains of the Peyto mansion, just a garden wall. But the arch is very beautiful and bears all the marks of the master. There are more than 40 different brick mouldings used in its fashioning, and these have now all had to be drawn so that a specialist firm can make the bricks to the moulds.

Recent archaeological excavation has revealed steps from the arch down the slope and into the field, although these have been entirely submerged for a century or so. The great sculptor Nicholas Stone was working on Peyto monuments within the church at the time the arch was built, and it is believed that he himself may well have supervised the construction work.

Sir Edward developed a reputation for seeking the best quality in all he did and, obviously delighted with the work of his friend Inigo Jones, he had him build for him a truly splendid windmill. It was originally intended to have been used as an observatory, since Sir Edward was a keen astronomer, but eventually it became a working windmill. The Chesterton

44

windmill is a noted landmark for miles around and dominates the sky line. Its lines are aesthetically perfect, supported as it is on six semi-circular moulded arches on piers. It has been repaired and altered since the time of Sir Edward and sadly at one stage it began to fall into disrepair. However, it always had many admirers and thanks to their representations, in 1965 it was completely and beautifully restored to its former glory by Warwickshire County Council under whose safe guardianship it still remains.

This windmill is unique but there is one other that bears some resemblance, and this is in Rhode Island, USA. It is thought that Benedict Arnold had this version built to his own rough drawings. He was born in Leamington Spa in 1615 and later emigrated to Rhode Island with his father. He would naturally have seen the construction of the Chesterton windmill as it progressed, and as a young man he may have become impressed by its superb proportions. Arnold became Governor of Rhode Island in 1663, and it is extremely likely that the Rhode Island structure was built in 1675, according to experts.

The Peyto family flourished, and eventually married into the Verney family, whose mansion Compton Verney is a mere half dozen miles away. In 1802 the then Lord Willoughby de Broke decided there was no need for two grand mansions so close to each other, and the curious mansion at Chesterton was sacrificed. Totally destroyed, its building materials were carted into Birmingham and sold. It took less than a generation for all trace to disappear.

The little church of St Giles, tucked well off the beaten track and scarce visible unless you knew it was there, contains many superb Peyto memorials and effigies, including the work of Nicholas Stone.

This first vicar of this church was John Lacy in 1414. It seems he must have been a man of some courage, for in 1415 when he had been but a year in office, he received Sir John Oldcastle, known as Lord Cobham and leader of the Lollards. Lacy must have known this man had been indicated for heresy, but he hid him, fed him and harboured him. Later he sued for and received the King's pardon for this deed.

Clifford Chambers

◣ Although only a couple of miles from Stratford-upon-Avon, Clifford Chambers used to be in Gloucestershire, a small island within Warwickshire, until boundary changes earlier this century regulated the situation. It belonged to the Abbey of St Peter in Gloucester, and was really Clifford Chamber*er* for it was here that the abbot stayed when he travelled.

Although well known, it is well hidden, for the main road through to Mickleton passes quite a way off and Clifford Chambers has the good fortune to be a true and natural cul-de-sac, with the end of its main street 'blocked' by Clifford Manor. The main street – indeed the only – is wide and green, with some timber-framed houses, and just off it a tiny square of ancient cottages.

The manor was once a fine moated medieval building, one of the best in these parts. In the 16th century it passed into the hands of the Rainsford family and they built themselves a more fashionable house, standing next to the old timbered grange used by the abbot of St Peter's. The Rainsfords were a family of some note and Lady Anne Rainsford was the daughter of Sir Henry Goodere of Polesworth, in the north of Warwickshire. In her father's house was a young poet, Michael Drayton, for Sir Henry was a patron of poets. Michael Drayton fell in love with the young Anne, although it seems she never returned his love, or perhaps didn't even know of it, and never regarded him as anything other than a dear friend of her childhood.

Michael Drayton, together with his friends William Shakespeare and Ben Jonson, was a frequent visitor to Clifford Manor, where he used to spend much of every summer. The Lady Anne crops up a great deal in his poetry and he refers to her home as 'the Muse's Quiet Port', and talks of 'Deere Clifford'. Once when staying with the Rainsfords, Drayton became ill with a 'tertian fever' and was cured by an emetic of syrup of violets administered by Dr John Hall of Stratford-upon-Avon, son-in-law to William Shakespeare.

Shakespeare knew Clifford well. When he was born in 1564, the old vicarage house at Clifford was the home of Mr John

Shakespeare, obviously of the same family, but what exact relation is not known. There were Shakespeare families in many Warwickshire villages. Mary Arden, and her husband John Shakespeare of Stratford-upon-Avon, had already lost two children shortly after their birth. William was their third child and first son. When he was but a few months old the dreaded plague came to Stratford, carried by Leicester's soldiers returning from war in the Low Countries. The disease' spread, and Mary Arden must have been terrified for the life of her tiny son. Many people left the town, seeking an escape, and it is thought that Mary Arden and the baby went to stay at Clifford with her husband's kinfolk until the danger within the town had abated.

The Rainsfords at Clifford Manor were staunch Royalists and during the Commonwealth their estate was seized by the State and given to the Dighton family. The too decided to make their house more fashionable and encased the old manor house with a Wren-type exterior round about the year 1700, leaving the timbered granary as it was.

In 1918 the whole house was gutted by a disastrous fire, and nothing remained but the bare brick walls. Edward Lutyens was commissioned to rebuild it and this he did, with great sensitivity, changing some of the interior but allowing much of the exterior to remain. The timbered grange had to be completely rebuilt, finer than the original, with interlaced beams and intricate king posts. Sometime during the 1950s when the building was bout to be listed, the whole thing was pulled down, leaving just the mansion house. It was described as an act of 'crass vandalism' and remains so. The gardens at the manor, after the fire, were laid out by Gertrude Jekyll, who so often worked with Lutyens. The house has since then suffered many vicissitudes and has for some time been an hotel.

Quite close to the manor, upon the banks of the river Stour, is Clifford Mill. It was here that a Hungarian, Mr Tibor Reich, came just after the end of the Second World War, to set up a textile design business. He experimented, gave employment to local people, and very soon his deep textures and colours were known all over the world. His fabrics were used in the new

Coventry Cathedral, and in many of the great ocean liners, including the *Queen Elizabeth II*.

Here in Clifford too, behind a house in the main street, are the glasshouses of the Woodfield brothers, specialists in lupins and delphiniums. The Woodfields exhibit every year at Chelsea and seldom come away without at least one gold medal. Here they create new varieties, named after the famous, and from here go many specimens to adorn the gardens of stately homes all over the country.

In the church there are some good tombs to the Rainsford family, as one might expect. But you will have to search the churchyard for a while to discover the tomb of Susanna Lovell, the 'Gipsy Queen'.

Compton Wynyates

◥ Not so much a hamlet as a cluster of dwellings around the most romantic house of its period, and probably one of the most photographed. Built in a deep hollow, enfolded in the gentle undulations of the hills, it is a warm red brick rambling mansion, with tall twisty chimneys wreathed in faint blue mist on fine summer mornings. Behind it stands Windmill Hill, topped by the strong sturdy mill that once served the area, its sails gleaming like silver in sunlight. This old mill was restored in the 1970s.

Nearby is the small church, no longer used for worship except on occasions, and a handful of cottages mostly occupied by those connected with the estate. In the churchyard is the grave of Jane Storey, the Compton witch, although she does not appear to have ever done anything very dreadful.

The great house of Compton Wynyates is no longer open to the public as it used to be, but is now the private home of the present Marquess of Northampton. It is, however, possible to stand on the side of the road and look down upon this truly serene and beautiful house, described by all the experts as the most perfect example of its period in the country. You would be

Compton Pike

well advised to look, for here is the stuff that dreams are made on.

On the opposite side of the road, on rising ground, is Compton Pike, a pyramid-shaped stone spire, one of many erected right across the country. In times long past, a signal fire would have been lighted atop this to send on news of important happenings. It is also thought that in particularly evil weather, a lighted faggot would have been fixed to the top of Compton Pike to guide any benighted travellers across the terrain, which was then open and wild waste.

Compton Wynyates has been the home of the Compton family since the 13th century, and the present house replaced a much earlier one on the same site. Most of the materials were carried here from Fulbrook, near Warwick, where a 'little castle of brick and stone' had been allowed to fall into ruin because the great Earl of Warwick didn't want another castle so close to his own.

The Comptons go back in the direct male line to Philip de Compton in 1204, but the foundations of their prosperity, and indeed their glory, were laid by William Compton. His father Edmund died in 1493, leaving young William only eleven years old and a ward of the Crown. The boy was appointed page to the two year old Prince Henry, who later became Henry VIII. Thus the young William and Henry became friends, until William Compton died in 1528 in an epidemic of the sweating sickness.

During those years of friendship, William Compton was never far from the King's side. He followed him to the Field of the Cloth of Gold and on his military expeditions, and after the victory at Tournai the King knighted him on the cathedral steps. He had many well deserved honours and riches given to him, and one of these was Fulbrook Castle, which he had permission to pull down to embellish his own home at Compton Wynyates.

King Henry VIII and his Queen Katherine of Aragon stayed many times at Compton, and one of the rooms was called 'Henry VIII's Room'. Its stained glass windows represented the arms of England and of Aragon. There was even 'King Harry's gilt bed'. In 1572 Queen Elizabeth I stayed here, and in her retinue was Lord Burleigh, who wrote to a friend 'surely the entertainment here is very great'.

The Comptons fought zealously and and with immense courage during the Civil War. Sir Spencer Compton, the 2nd Earl, had three of his sons with him at the Battle of Edgehill and all were knighted on the field. On 19th March 1643 the Earl was killed at the Battle of Hopton Heath. He had two sons with him, James and Charles, who after the battle sought the body of their father. The Parliamentarians refused to part with it, except the Comptons return to them the eight guns they had captured. So the eight guns were given up, and the brave Earl's body carried home for burial. He could have saved his own life, but had angrily declared he 'scorned to take quarter from such base rogues and rebels'.

50

In June 1644 Compton Wynyates was captured by the Parliamentarians. The widow of Spencer, the 2nd Earl, was still living in the house with her youngest son, but she seems to have been as brave as her husband, for unknown to the Puritan Colonel Purefoy, wounded Royalists were hidden in the roof space. The good lady secretly and at dead of night crept up there to attend to them.

The rebels drove the deer from the park, defaced the monuments in the church, then flung them into the moat. They took 120 prisoners, £5,000 in money, 60 horses, 400 sheep, 160 head of cattle and 18 cartloads of plunder. This done, they demolished the church. It was rebuilt in 1665, and as many of the monuments taken from the moat and replaced as possible.

The following January, the Comptons raised a force of 300 men and stormed Compton Wynyates in an attempt to get their home back, but despite the fact they took the enemy unawares, cut down the drawbridge and killed the sentinels, they were not successful and were driven back. Meanwhile, Sir William, son of the 2nd Earl, busied himself raising more forces and attempting a rescue of the King from the Tower. After the war was over, they recovered Compton Wynyates by paying a heavy fine, and Cromwell ordered that the moat around the house be filled in and battlements removed.

They were colourful, larger than life people, the Comptons, and they didn't brook any denial once they had made up their minds on a course of action. In 1559 William, 2nd Lord Compton, got his chosen bride by a very unusual method. He fell in love with Elizabeth, the only child of the very rich London merchant, Sir John Spencer. Sir John would have none of William, but he reckoned without that young man's determination. Sir William bribed the local baker to allow him to deliver bread to the Spencer household in Canonbury. He entered the house dressed as a baker, bearing a large basket full of loaves. He left the house, but crouched on the bottom of the empty basket was his beloved Elizabeth, covered over with a white cloth. So off they went, and were married. Sir John Spencer refused to be reconciled and disowned the pair of them.

One day, however, he received a message from Queen Elizabeth that she wished him to stand sponsor with her at the baptism of an infant. Sir John was very sensible of the honour the Queen did him, and could do nothing but agree. Accordingly, he turned up at the appointed hour, doubtless clad in his very best, only to find the smiling Queen ready to present, and stand godmother to, his very first grandson. Naturally, it all ended happily ever after.

There is still in existence a letter which Elizabeth Spencer wrote to her young husband, William Compton, round about the time of their marriage. In it she lists in great detail all the monies he is to make available to her, how many new gowns she is to have per year, how many horses, how many waiting women, how many carriages are to be for her exclusive use, how many new jewels, and how often, and how much money she will need to perform charitable works as becomes her station in life. She seems as equally determined as Sir William, and she does not stint herself. Presumably Sir William acceded to her requests.

The Comptons' fortunes fluctuated as did those of any other great family, but in 1768 they were very nearly completely ruined by gambling, and by a recklessly expensive and foolish Parliamentary election campaign in Northampton. In 1774 the contents of the lovely old house at Compton Wynyates were sold off by auction for whatever they would fetch, including 'King Harry's gilt bed' which went for £10. Lord Northampton sold off the timber and almost everything else that would raise money, and went off to live in Switzerland, after telling his steward at Compton Wynyates, John Berrill, to pull the house down.

Poor John Berrill. He had been steward for many years and he loved Compton Wynyates. How could his master tell him to pull it down? He couldn't bring himself to do it and, for the first time in his life, he disobeyed. He contented himself with blocking up all the windows, and stopping up the holes in the roof to keep out the worst of the weather, and he just bided his time, hoping that one day the Comptons would return to this most lovely house.

And they did, round about 1812, when the then Lord Northampton arrived unexpectedly and struggled around his almost ruined home, peering by the light of candles. He promptly set about restoring it to its former glory, and how glad steward John Berrill must have been. The Compton family has since been thankful that their good and faithful servant did, just once, disobey an instruction. John Berrill died in 1834, and is buried in Compton Wynyates church, beneath a plain stone slab.

Comptons continue at Compton Wynyates. Looking at this serene spot, it is difficult to visualise how it once rang with cannon fire; the pomp and ceremonial that it must have seen when visited by Henry Viii, Queen Elizabeth and James I. The pageants, entertainments, throngs of bright coloured courtiers. If ever walls were indeed 'stone tapes' then I would like to listen to those of the rose red brick of Compton Wynyates.

Cubbington

The 'new' part of this village lies close to Leamington Spa, but diligent searchers may penetrate further into the older part, down a pleasant leafy byway. Here old houses are grouped around the church, inside which is a memorial to Abraham Murcott, mariner, who served with Sir Cloudesley Shovel and who lost his life when his ship, laden with gold dust, hit storm conditions just off the Isles of Scilly. Almost home, but not quite.

One of Cubbington's most notable rectors was Rev James Austen, brother of novelist Jane Austen, who lived here from 1792 until 1820. It is highly likely that his sister Jane visited him, for it is known she often stayed in Warwickshire at Stoneleigh Abbey just a few miles off, with her relations, the Leighs.

One of Warwickshire's famous Greswolde family created something of a stir if not a scandal in 1635. Edward Greswolde was a man of strange religious convictions, which he carried through to the letter, it seems. He may have been suffering from some form of mental illness, and this could have been worsened by the fact that this elder brother had been 'set aside' and Edward made heir, when he knew in his heart of hearts that he should not have inherited.

Edward Greswolde was so firmly of the belief that he must have no truck with sinners, or use anything of man's invention, that he shut himself and his children up inside his house, with no food or comforts. Food was put through a hole in the wall by those kindly disposed, but eventually as time wore on, and the food was not taken in, neighbours became very seriously concerned. They could hear no noise, no movement. They had seen no one, not even the slightest suspicion of anyone for months, and the Justices of the Peace were informed. They forced entry into the house and found Mr Greswolde lying very ill and near to death upon his bed. Two of his children were already dead and had been so for a long time, for their bodies were decomposed and corrupted.

He had mutilated his only book, his Bible, so that all the titles given by man had been cut out, leaving only the text which he believed to be God's word. Alas, poor Mr Greswolde. After his death, and that of all his children, the estate reverted back to the man who should have had it in the first place, the brother who had been set aside.

Of sterner stuff was another famous Cubbington resident, Joseph Russell, inventor, innovator and author. He was born relatively humble circumstances, one of the 17 children of the village blacksmith at nearby Ashow in 1760. After only twelve months' education in Birmingham, and when he was but 20 years old, he settled in Cubbington in 1780 as a tenant farmer, with 320 acres of waste and heath, enough to daunt most other people before they start!

His neighbours were astonished when he first planted four acres of Bericote Wood with asparagus, which he then supplied fresh cut to the lucrative markets in nearby towns. He extended this operation as years went on. He also grew another crop upon which he founded a small industry. Acres of flax were grown, and this was dressed and spun on an outwork basis in surrounding villages. When this was successfully established he built a mill for the bleaching, and employed 100 hands. One year his entire crop was destroyed by fire, and three valuable horses employed upon the flax business were drowned in a sudden freak flood.

Joseph Russell introduced Leicester sheep into Warwickshire, and experimented with cross breeding. He imported a new strain of wheat, Talavera, into this country for the first time in 1810. He was an improver of the sub-soil plough, and invented a new machine for gathering clover heads. For this he was honoured by the Society of Arts and Sciences in London, and he began to write of his experiments and discoveries. In 1830 he published *A Treatise on the Practice of Chemical Agriculture*, quite a revolutionary document in its time. This was followed by *Observations on the Growth of British Corn* some two years later.

His neighbours took an interest in his activities, and began to put some of his findings to good use. Joseph Russell was always ready and willing to help and advise, for he had the cause of the farmers and of agriculture very much at heart. He had 17 children, of whom 14 survived. Joseph Russell went on discovering and writing to the end of his life, and died aged 86 in Kenilworth, where he was living with one of his daughters.

Edstone

Warwickshire has certainly bred some eccentrics over the years, and thank goodness for that. One of these was the rollicking, rumbustical, merry Squire of Edstone Hall, William Somervile. He was a man of letters, friend of the famous dedicated follower of all field sports, and such a wonderful host that no one ever refused an invitation to his table. Edstone Hall still stands, well hidden behind trees and high walls on the main A34 Stratford-upon-Avon to Birmingham road, not far from Wootton Wawen. The present house, however, is not the comfortable, roomy two-storey thatched structure of Somervile's halcyon days.

The Somerviles were an ancient family long settled in Gloucestershire, until Thomas Somervile married Joan Aylesbury of Edstone and brought the property into the family. Thomas died in 1500 but the Somerviles continued at Edstone, although in 1583 it was nearly lost to them forever.

John Somervile married Margaret, a kinswoman of the Ardens, Shakespeare's mother's family, and he became afflicted by a 'frantic humour' as it was described. Egged on by the powerful Arden clan and by their priest Hugh Hall, who lived in the house disguised as a servant, John Somervile set off to London to kill the Queen, Elizabeth I. He made no secret of his plan, and said it was because of the plight of the Catholic fraternity. He was arrested at Aynho and flung into the Tower. All concerned with this infamous plot were rounded up, tried and rapidly sentenced to death, but John Somervile cheated the gallows by hanging himself in his cell, so they had to content themselves with sticking his head upon a spike on London Bridge as a warning to all who might plot against the Queen. His estates at Edstone were seized by the Crown, since he was attainted with treason. But it was discovered that he had not yet come to his 24th birthday, and thus hadn't technically inherited. So Edstone escaped and passed to John's brother, who very sensibly kept his head down for the next few years.

Into this family in the year 1680 or thereabouts was born William, eldest of six sons. He received his early education in Stratford and then went to Winchester College, scraping in by the skin of his teeth as 'founder's kin' through his maternal grandmother, a member of the Fiennes family of Broughton Castle, near Banbury. Neither at Winchester, nor later at Oxford, did Somervile show any aptitude for scholarship, and when his father died he was overjoyed to be able to return to Edstone and assume the mantle of a country squire. He married Mary Bethel in 1708, and although the marriage was a happy one, there were no children.

William Somervile's love of field sports amounted to a passion. He loved the countryside, loved food and wine, loved congenial company, liked nothing better than to have his house full and his table crowded, and he loved a wager.

It was said of him that he paid more attention to his kennels than to his house, and with some truth. He kept twelve couple of beagles, bred chiefly between the small Cotswold harrier and the Southern hound, six couple of fox hounds, and five couple of otter hounds. The feeding, breeding and total management he attended to personally, and conducted the chase as well. His favourite old horse became a legend throughout the county; a typical English hunter, 15 hands, short back, big barrel, and known as Old Ball.

Somervile was a handsome man, well built and with a mane of blonde hair. He took his squirearchy very seriously and conscientiously attended to all his public duties. He had no idea of money management, and was permanently financially embarrassed. In the last years of his life Somervile gave one of his many and famous dinner parties, some 200 guests seated around his table. The company grew convivial, and none more so than the host. Wagers flew, and Somervile bet £50 that he would be up, kill his hares and pick them up before any of the young bloods present. He did it and won with ease.

Many knowledgeable people have argued about his poetry. Certainly his most famous work *The Chase* is said to be good because it was written with the whole heart of a true follower of the chase, rather than a mere poet watching from the sidelines. Dr Johnson, that slightly irascible commentator upon most things, said Somervile 'wrote well for a gentleman...'.

The Chase was followed by *Hobbinol* a kind of rural burlesque dedicated by Somervile to the painter Hogarth. Another burlesque, *The Wicker Chair*, was written in the kitchen of a farmhouse, while between horses out hunting. The year he died, 1742, saw the publication of a massive work, *Field Sports*, in which he included hawking, shooting and fishing, subjects upon which he was an acknowledged master. His death was lamented, for he was probably one of the most loved, the most jolly, the most kindly and most likeable characters in the county.

Two of Somervile's huntsmen lie buried in Wootton Wawen church. The grave of James Boeter bears a Latin inscription, written by Somervile, describing him as 'faithful within doors and without'. Boeter died from a fall off a horse while out hunting with Somervile in January 1719. The other one, John Hoitt, however, lived to be 89. He entered Somervile's service as a lad of twelve, and scarce left his side until his master's death. Hoitt's epitaph, written by the vicar of that time, says:

> Here Hoitt, all his sport and labours past
> Joins his loved master Somervile at last
> Together they went, echoing fields to try
> Together now in silent dust they lie.

Somervile as one may well expect, wrote his own epitaph long before it was likely to be required. He loved words, loved language, and probably wanted to ensure he got what he wanted. It has a slight 'tongue in cheek' ring about it:

> If in me thou has found aught of good – imitate it
> If aught of evil – avoid it with all thy strength
> Trust in Christ and know that thou also are frail
> and mortal.

He died as he had lived, in debt, and his estate passed to a cousin. But how Somervile had lived, and how much he had enjoyed his life. His poetry is no longer fashionable, but who knows, it may eventually be taken up once more; someone might recognise through it how much Somervile loved his native heath, his hounds, his home and his friends.

Ettington

Just outside the village of Ettington, close by a busy traffic roundabout, there stand the ruins of a church. Roughly handled by wind and weather, all that remains is the creepy, slightly Gothick tower amid a churchyard overgrown with grass, encroaching brambles, and trees leaning drunkenly towards broken monuments.

The church was built in 1794 and rapidly acquired the reputation for being the ugliest church in the whole of country. So Ettington shamefacedly discarded it and built another one, half a mile down the main street. The old church, dedicated to

Ettington old church

St Thomas a Becket, fell into disrepair and was pulled down in 1902, leaving only the tower.

It was in this lost and lonely place that the victim of a local murder was buried with scant ceremony on a dark November evening in 1897, although now there is noting to mark this particular grave from any other of the sunken mounds. The murder aroused great feeling at the time, so much so that in the press it became known as 'The Ettington Sensation'.

The Brandish family were local, and the eldest son George,

with his wife Louisa and their five children, lived at Drybank Farm, about a mile south of the village. The farm still exists, although now it is a bit less lonely since a busy road passes quite close by. George Brandish was obviously a good man, well respected, and worked as a bailiff to Mr Jeffery Lowe, a man of Quaker persuasion living at the Hall.

George had a sister, Elizabeth, a nurse who moved about the Midlands, employed by local ladies committees to undertake care of the sick and to cope with confinements. She was, I suppose, the forerunner of the District Nurse. In between jobs, she returned to Ettington, staying at Drybank Farm with her brother and his family. They were very friendly and Elizabeth seems to have been able to come and go as she chose.

Sometime in 1895 Elizabeth Brandish, secretly and alone, gave birth to an illegitimate child, a boy, whom she called Rees Thomas Yells Brandish. No one ever knew who his father was, for Elizabeth kept her secret very closely. Even George and Louisa knew nothing of the child's existence. It is believed the boy was born in Kent, for Nurse Brandish put him with foster parents in Ashford, using the name 'Mrs Edwards' and for the next two years she paid five shillings a week for his keep, although she did not see him.

Quite suddenly, when little Rees was about two and a half years old, 'Mrs Edwards' arrived in Ashford to collect her child. The foster parents were very upset, for they had heard no word from her, and they had grown very fond of the little boy. 'Mrs Edwards' would brook no denial, and she took little Rees unwillingly away with her. She promised the foster parents she would write to them and let them know how the child fared. She told them he would be happy with her brother's children in Ettington, a place they hadn't heard of. The foster parents kissed the child for the last time.

No letter came, and the foster parents became anxious. They recalled the name of the village, Ettington, and accordingly and laboriously penned a letter addressed simply to the vicar of Ettington. When the vicar received it, he could make neither head nor tail of the affair. He knew nothing of a child called 'Rees' or of a 'Mrs Edwards'. He handed the letter on to the police, who immediately became alarmed at the supposed disappearance of a child and began investigations.

Eventually Nurse Brandish was arrested working in Clent, not far from Birmingham, but she absolutely refused to tell the police anything at all. The search for the little boy went on for nine weeks, with every pond, ditch, hedgerow, coppice and bit of woodland around Ettington being thoroughly dragged or beaten, but to no avail.

George Brandish was bewildered. He knew nothing of any child, he said, and he spoke the truth. Eventually, only one place remained to be searched. The garden at Drybank Farm. It was decided it must be entirely dug over, and a stalwart body of policemen from Kineton and from Shipston turned up to do the job. Armed with spades, they started in, and then one of them astutely noticed there was something not quite right with a row of recently planted cabbages. A few of the plants right in the middle of the row appeared to be sprinkled with lime, while the rest did not. They dug into the middle of the cabbages, and it was not long before they came upon the decomposing body of little Rees Brandish, within nine feet of the front windows of his uncle's house.

It was discovered that Nurse Brandish had got on the train at Ashford with her son. When she eventually got off the train at Ettington station (this was in the days when it did have a railway station) she had no child with her, only a large tin box so heavy she required help with it. The local carrier took her and the tin box to Drybank Farm.

There was some doubt, after several inquests, about the cause of the child's death since his body was so decomposed, and forensic science was not then as sophisticated as it is today, but it was decided he had been suffocated.

It was subsequently revealed that while working in Clent, Elizabeth Brandish had begun a relationship with the local policeman, Sergeant Narramore, a widower with two daughters. She hoped to marry him. He knew nothing of her guilty secret and she knew only too well that if the truth came out, he would not marry her. Even if he wanted to, it was not likely that he would have been allowed to; police rules in 1897 were extremely strict.

Elizabeth Brandish appeared at Warwick Assizes in March 1898, but the jury failed to reach the required unanimous verdict. She appeared again in July of that year, when a sympathetic jury decided she had 'suffered enough' and she was acquitted, to the fairly loudly expressed indignation of a crowded court room.

Poor little Rees Brandish, the innocent victim of this tangle, was buried as secretly as he had been born. He was illegitimate, and it was not known whether he had ever been baptised, so no clergyman attended. The undertaker's men simply put the little body in a plain coffin and took it up to the churchyard of the ugliest church in the country, under cover of darkness. These circumstances gave rise to further outbursts of indignation in the local press, who described it as a pathetic ending to a short sad little life.

So somewhere in this forgotten churchyard lies little Rees Brandish. But at least wild flowers blow about him.

Exhall

Here we have the 'Dodging Exhall' of Shakespeare's rhyme, thought to be a reference to the fact that in his day this village really was inaccessible. There was no direct road to it until after the Enclosure Acts, and even now you have to know where it is, but when you get there it is well worth it. Although only six miles from the town of Stratford-upon-Avon, it retains an air of remoteness, a flavour of being content to remain hidden.

Most of the cottages are brick and timber, and these have stood four square to the elements for a century or so. There is some stone, which came from quarries in the adjoining parishes of Grafton and Binton. These have long since closed down, but fossils discovered in them are on view at the County Museum in Warwick.

The houses of Exhall are built high upon banks, and experts have speculated to no avail for years about how the main road of Exhall was formed. It meanders, with the banks on either side so steep in places it has a slight resemblance to a cutting. A large boulder in a roadside bank is thought to be a glacier stone, but for generations Exhall children have called it the 'growing stone', It is so called in old school log books, and is said to have increased in size over the years. Those who sit upon it are said to grow, but no one is sure whether this refers to their physical size or their intellect. Legend has it that Shakespeare, having discovered 'Dodging Exhall' sat upon the growing stone and composed his four line rhyme.

One of the most notable residents of Exhall was John Walsingham, cousin to Sir Francis Walsingham, Secretary of State to Queen Elizabeth I. Not that Exhall's John Walsingham was involved in affairs of the court. He seems to have been perfectly content to remain at home with his wife Elenor and his mother, Elizabeth.

There is a very beautiful brass to John and Elenor Walsingham in the little village church of St Giles. He wears armour of the period and has closely cropped hair, a moustache and beard. and she is dressed in a French hood, neck ruff and farthingale. John died in 1566, but the date of Elenor's death has been left blank.

It is thought they might have once lived in Exhall Court, although this is by no means certain. There was an old house upon the site, and in 1855 it was demolished and a new house built by Hemming James Bomford, an agricultural engineer and farmer. The Bomford family remained at Exhall Court until 1976, and had their main works a few miles up the road, which became, of course, Bomford and Evershed.

The church of St Giles was almost rebuilt in 1862 and almost everything of any age was whisked away. The Walsingham brass was somehow saved, although the table tomb upon which it rested was removed. The brass is upon the floor in a dark corner of the chancel.

Another flat and ancient stone in the chancel has gone too, but a handwritten note inside the church tells us about it. It was in memory of Rev Richard Wright, rector 1625-1650, a very troubled period. His epitaph, written in Latin, described him as a pastor, a physician of souls and bodies, who 'in the bestowal of his goods, the irksomeness of a prison, the sequestration of his benefices, and the endurance of many afflictions, happily proved with unflinching courage against all the indictments of seditious men, his faithfulness to GOD, the KING and the CHURCH'. He died on 31st December 1650 and his dutiful daughter, Lady Anne Warmstry, got her husband, the Dean of Worcester, to write her father's epitaph. The dean was not able to do much about it until 1661, when he was engaged in repairing the ravages wrought by the Puritans in Worcester Cathedral.

Outside is a tomb to Rev Thomas Keyt, another suffering clergyman, for it tells us he died at the age of 71, after being deprived of his living because he refused to take the oath to King William and Queen Mary. He was once the rector of nearby Binton, but was almost certainly driven out by the usual religious bigotry.

One of Exhall's more successful rectors was Dr William Thomas (1698-1723) for it was he who completely revised and brought up to date Sir William Dugdale's *Antiquities of Warwickshire*, a monumental task which Dr Thomas completed in 1730 and he presented a copy to his former parish of Exhall. They, very sensibly, later deposited it with the County Record Office for safe keeping.

Inside the church, I found a friendly local lady putting fresh spring flowers into a brass vase dedicated to her mother. Mrs Fanny Reeves died in 1965 at the age of 74 and was much revered in Exhall, for she held the post of verger to 'her' church faithfully for 55 years. A record that has not yet been beaten.

Flecknoe

A truly well hidden piece of Warwickshire, for only by the signposts do you know of its existence. It used to be just a tiny part of the much larger parish of Wolfhamcote, together with Nethercote and Sawbridge, but now Flecknoe is the only village left, clustered around the slopes of Bush Hill, the highest point in this corner of the county, rising to some 500 ft. It is thought that the old windmill recorded in 16th century documents must have stood upon its summit.

Wolfhamcote has entirely disappeared, except for its church and nearby manor house. The church fell into complete disrepair and looked a pitiful sight with its broken windows, sitting alone in the middle of fields. But it was rescued by the Friendless Churches Fund, and is now very neat and tidy, except that it is kept locked.

Sir Christopher Hatton used to own Wolfhamcote, given to him by Queen Elizabeth I, and it was rumoured that their friendship was a fairly warm one! Certainly they wrote many letters to each other, and the Queen called Sir Christopher 'my mutton' or 'my bellwether'. It could be that these were fashionable terms of endearment in Tudor times, but as Wolfhamcote was depopulated in order to go in for the extremely profitable rearing of sheep, they do sound singularly apt.

Nethercote, once called 'Little Flecknoe' or 'Flecknoe Parva' is no more. Here too, its peasants were turned off rich grazing land so that sheep might be moved in. Excavations carried out in this whole area in 1955 proved that it was once an established and thriving settlement, dating from before the Romans came to our shores.

Sawbridge too is gone, all except for its manor house. There was an extraordinary find here in 1689 when a man called John Eales, a modest farmer, decided to remove an old barn. Beneath it he found a well, in good order, measuring some four foot square, which he had not known was there. He fetched some help and began to investigate. Some feet below they found a large stone, an set upon the stone were twelve Roman urns, grey in colour and 'curiously polished'. With some difficulty they got them out, but several got broken in the process.

They then turned their attention to the stone upon which the urns had rested and noticed that it had a hole bored all the way through it. They attempted to shift the stone, but discovered it went down some 20 ft. Below it was a great deal of water, and the well rapidly and alarmingly narrowed. Wisely, they decided to leave it alone. What happened to all the curious Roman urns is not known, except that a man called Thomas Clarke, a gentleman of Wolfhamcote who had come along to see what went on, decided to take several for himself.

Whilst its neighbours have slowly but inexorably disappeared, Flecknoe has modestly expanded. It is an attractive village, quiet and secluded, and now boasts a Flecknoe Society which aims to keep a watchful eye upon developments. It has a fine inn with the unusual name of the Old Olive Bush, a village hall which a few of the residents are raising money to continually improve, and a tiny church of St Mark, built in 1891. It has no outstanding architectural features, but doubtless the inhabitants of Flecknoe got a bit fed up with struggling down the rough track to Wolfhamcote, and decided that self-help was no bad thing.

Flecknoe must have slumbered away for many years, until it suffered a rude awakening in 1939 when a war-time camp appeared on its very doorstep. A couple of the rather ugly camp buildings still remain on one of the farms.

Perhaps Flecknoe felt the ravages of the sheep rearing period, for when Joseph Arch began to hold meetings which later led to the formation of an Agricultural Labourer's Union in February 1872, the Flecknoe men were among the first to make their views known.

Gaydon

In the 18th century, the rough roads of Warwickshire were a lucrative source of income for highwaymen and gangs of robbers who lay in wait for the unsuspecting traveller. The main Warwick to Banbury road was no exception, and it was at the Gaydon Inn on that main route that the notorious Culworth gang met and divided their spoils. The Gaydon Inn still remains, now venerable and amiable, offering traditional hospitality to travellers.

The Culworth gang terrorised the whole neighbourhood on the borders of Warwickshire, Oxfordshire and Northamptonshire for almost 20 years before they were finally caught and paid the penalty. The gang comprised some 15 men, all of whom lived in surrounding villages. The ringleader, John Smith, lived in the village of Culworth, just in Northants, and he and his two sons, John and William, formed the nucleus of the gang.

It all started off fairly modestly, with just a bit of poaching. John Smith, although getting on in years, was said to possess enormous strength and was quite fearless, although he seems to have been very well able to generate fear both among his followers and his victims. His sons were completely under his thumb. Another member of the gang was the parish clerk who so far forgot himself as to carry a pistol beneath his clerical gown.

Soon it was decided poaching was not enough, and the gang took to robbery. One of their trademarks was that they always blacked their faces and wore smock frocks to do their robberies. More and more daring became their raids, and although neighbours were suspicious, and many locals knew who the gang were, they were too afraid to say.

The gang laid their plans well. They robbed coaches travelling from Warwick to Banbury, and vice versa, but they never appeared in the same place twice. Then they got a bit careless, and it was the beginning of the end when the landlord of an inn in Northamptonshire became suspicious of two men who asked for a room one dark winter evening. When they were asleep, he crept into the room and searched their bags, finding smock frocks and valuable.s He called in the law, and the gang was more or less finished at that moment.

John Smith, the leader, was sentenced to be hanged, and in his last days in gaol he wrote to his wife urging her to tell their two sons to learn a lesson from his better end and to henceforth tread the straight and narrow path. He also commanded that John Smith should marry the girl with whom he had been 'keeping company', Elizabeth Beere.

William took his father's warning to heart, and when he came out of gaol went to work on a local farm, where he lived a blameless life for the next 20 years. John, however, went the other way and became a notorious highwayman, with his main beat the road between Warwick and Banbury. This was where he was finally caught, close to the Gaydon Inn, where he was locked in an upper room for the night. He whiled away his time by carving his name upon a beam.

He was tried at Warwick, where his glib tongue availed him naught, and was sentenced to death by hanging. His sweetheart, Elizabeth Beere, was present at the trial and in the cold light of dawn a couple of days later, witnessed the hanging. She watched as her lover's body was hoisted high on the gallows, and when he was cut down she begged to be allowed to take his body home with her.

The lifeless corpse of John Smith was flung across the back of a donkey, and Elizabeth Beere walked the long road back from Warwick, leading the creature along the same notorious highway that had been her lover's downfall, past the Gaydon Inn where he had spent his last night of felony, with his body jerking and jolting about on the animal's back. She saw to it that he was decently buried, and with him died her hopes of marriage to the man she so obviously loved.

Great Wolford

Just beyond the parish of Great Wolford, as the road wends its way towards Moreton-in-Marsh (or Moreton Henmarsh in the old records), stands the Four Shires Stone. It once marked the boundaries of four shires, Gloucestershire, Warwickshire, Worcestershire and Oxfordshire. However, since the powers that be have since moved the county boundaries more than once, this is no longer the case.

The area used to be known as Wolford Heath but there is little now remaining of the wide open and rolling tracts of land, and the main road between Moreton-in-Marsh and Chipping Norton runs close by.

The stone is a large square edifice, composed of white oolite limestone believed to have been brought from the quarries around the Chipping Campden area, which is only a few miles away. It has a bit of the classical and a touch of the medieval

The Four Shire Stone

about it. Although its original date is not known, experts put it as late 16th century, and it has undoubtedly been added to and subtracted from over the centuries, with a four-faced sundial being added in the 18th century when embellishment was all the fashion. On the south-west side of the stone is 'Worcestershire'; on the north-west, 'Gloucestershire'; the north-east 'Warwickshire' and the south-east 'Oxfordshire'. It has no other word to say. The original round ball on the top was replaced by the Victorians, but then the replacement was stolen some years ago and was in turn replaced by a round ball of concrete.

When it was first erected, the stone would have stood isolated and provided any traveller struggling across the heath with a landmark for which to aim. Now buildings and roads have come ever closer to it, and iron railings have been put around it.

Needless to say, people throughout the ages have been busy carving their initials and dates upon the stone, as far up as a human being of reasonably average height can reach. So many have there been they have crossed and recrossed each other so that in many cases they are now totally illegible. What human hand has left undone, wind and weather has completed.

Halford

A few miles north of Shipston-on-Stour, the village of Halford sits across the much used Fosse Way. A few years ago this road was much narrower, and meandered at its leisure across a lovely old packhorse bridge that crossed the river Stour. The bridge was first mentioned in local records in 1278, and in 1633 was described as 'a great bridge and very useful to passengers going from Warwick unto Shipston. . .' . Ten years later, it was the scene of a skirmish between Royalists and Parliamentarians, and the bridge was deliberately broken down to prevent either side getting over the river.

However, things change. A decade or so ago, the County Council altered the line of the road so that it now pursues a straight course and is wide enough for the lorries that come hurtling through. The old packhorse bridge is cut off, down what has turned itself into something resembling a lay-by. It is still used by pedestrians and youngsters who want to fish with a bit of string and a bent pin.

Alongside the bridge is an ancient coaching inn, for centuries known as the Bell and a recognised meeting place for serious legal business. Those involved arrived by coach and stayed over at the Bell. Many old records, including several of the Enclosure Acts, show they were signed at 'the Bell at Hawford ...'. Now the inn has been refurbished to bring it more in line with current fashion, and has even been given a new name, the Halford Bridge Inn.

On the opposite side of the road is the bowling green, the oldest and probably the loveliest in the county, if not the Midlands. The old club house belonging to the Bell used to have a cockpit above it, where in the past men would lay bets upon the prowess of their birds. It would seem that all the leisure activities of Halford were thus easily taken into account a couple of centuries ago. Now the ancient cockpit has gone, leaving no trace. The bowling club, how ever, has a new clubhouse and the game still goes on as it has done for the past 400 years or more.

The major part, and the most delightful part, of this village cannot be seen from the main road, for it is well hidden round a curvy loop of twisty lanes behind the inn. Below the garden of the old manor you can still detect traces of where the ford used to be, a safe place to cross the Stour before the old packhorse bridge was built. A mound in the garden, rapidly diminishing, is where a small castle used to stand, doubtless built to defend the ford and ward off all those who boded no good.

The church of St Mary is tucked away down a side lane, and for those who delight in the beauty of ancient parish churches, this one is well worth a visit. It has a Norman tympanum, surrounding an extraordinary piece of Norman sculpture thought to rank among the finest of its kind. It is a seated figure with outspread wings, the arms holding a scroll and drapery flowing from the wrists.

The church has three bells, one dating from 1320, the oldest inscribed bell throughout the Midland counties. It also has the old fire hooks still hanging upon the walls. These were used in pre-brigade days for pulling down burning thatch to prevent flames from spreading. It took several able-bodied strong men to handle one and was no easy task, but doubtless served its purpose well. Most of the village used to be thatched, and some of it still is!

Within the church are the rather lovely memorials composed by one of Halford's historic vicars, the Rev George Grainger, a Puritan minister, who stoutly refused to affix his signature to the Loyal Address to Queen Anne after the Battle of Blenheim in 1704. George Grainger was inducted to the living of Halford in 1660, a few months after his marriage to Frances Savage of Meon, Lower Quinton. Seven children were born to them, and the eldest, Thomas Grainger, was a subscriber to the new 1730 edition of Dugdale's *Antiquities of Warwickshire* revised by Dr William Thomas.

The Rev George was something of a poet, and made verses upon the deaths of several members of his family. Some of the verses serve as epitaphs within or without the church, and some are to be found in the registers. They do have a certain style, and more than one researcher has wondered if somewhere there is a little collection of Grainger's work awaiting discovery.

Upon his father, John Grainger, who died in September 1673, he wrote

> He living lov'd a flow'r that here doth lie
> The embleme of his owne mortalitie

referring to the old custom of putting flowers inside the coffin rather than on the top of it as we do today. But his best verses were reserved for his wife, Frances, who died on 14th April 1674. *Threnodia in Defunctam* is in Latin, but the English translation gives us:

> She was a modest Virgin and a wife
> Chaste to her husband in the married life

A mirrour of her Sex, a Mother deare
Mild to good children, to the bad severe.
A decent Matron in her garb, her dresse
Neither fantastique or yet fashionlesse
Her carriage sober, of an holy mind
And open hand, her speech to all was kind
Her fame deserves in Marble to remaine
Born of a Gen'rous stocke & borne again.

This was inscribed with the date of her burial in the registers. On her stone we have

Thy body's for a moment here in dust
As in a cabinet repos'd
Until the hasting day enclos'd
Left to our mother earth in trust.

Her wall monument:

She sleeps in dust whose blest remaines survive
Which none doe know by those that godly live.

There is yet another verse to his infant daughter Aliasha, who died at three months, and is buried with her mother. And of himself, the good reverend gentleman says:

Lately I was, now here I lie
Taking my last repose in dust
Secure from paine and misery
From trouble care and lust
I have my Dormitory with the just.

There is a rather quaint tale of a baby pool at Halford. A small stream running through private gardens is known as Holy Go. It comes from a spring about a mile off, and trickles its way through to the Stour. The old legend has it that unwanted babies were first baptised in the pool, and then drowned within it. It was also thought to have healing properties and was excellent for bathing sore eyes. But the Holy Go pool has passed into the unknown, and the name only is perpetuated in the name of Holego House.

Haseley

A small corner tucked well out of sight, visited only by those who seek it out. Despite the fact that a busy road runs but a mile or two away, it still manages to remain an oasis of peace and quiet, with narrow, gently curving lanes, abutted by small fields and hedgerows.

It is a scattered hamlet, with a few houses near the old church and a few later ones clustered together at the other end, known as Haseley Knob. It was once a much larger village and the remains of the deserted medieval settlement may still be seen behind the present manor.

The manor of Haseley belonged in the 13th century to Thomas de Cherlecote. We do not know what kind of man this Thomas was, except that he offended against the King's Justices in some way and was fined. However, many people were fined for fairly minor offences in those days. Then, in 1263, Thomas de Cherlecote was found dead in a pool close by Haseley, known as Fletchers Hole. It was assumed he had committed suicide by drowning himself, and as suicide was not only a sin but a crime which must needs be punished, all Thomas de Cherlecote's lands and possessions were instantly seized by the Crown, leaving his son and heir with nothing. Then the full truth came out, and it was discovered that the unfortunate Thomas had been strangled by three of his servants, two men and one woman, who had thrown his lifeless body into the hole. They were rounded up, tried, and promptly executed.

The Crown relinquished the estates it had so promptly seized to Thomas de Cherlecote's son and heir, also Thomas, who was knighted, made one of the Commissioners for conservation of the peace, and made Sheriff of Warwickshire and Leicestershire. He was also advised to pay out monies for prayers to be said for the health of his murdered father's soul. Indeed, this Thomas did quite well, and had several grants and honours from the Crown, which must have been a great relief to him after being rendered virtually penniless and homeless.

In 1302 his son Robert sold Haseley to the Earl of Warwick, and in 1553 it came into the possession of Clement Throckmorton, third son of Sir George Throckmorton of Coughton Court, near Alcester. Clement built himself a fine Tudor house, the fragments of which may still be seen. He married Katherine Nevill, and they had a large family. Above the old porchway which he had built in 1561 is a Latin verse which translated gives us 'Here we have no continuing City but seek one to come'. There are also the initials 'C.T.' and 'K.T.' with true-lovers knots. Near the 'C.T.' is an olive branch with six shoots signifying six sons, and near the 'K.T.' another olive branch with seven shoots signifying seven daughters.

Around 1588 the country was set by the ears when brilliant and illegal Puritan pamphlets began to be circulated. These tracts protested in no uncertain manner about the direction the Church of England was taking. They were obviously illegal, perhaps even treasonable, and the search was on to find out who wrote them and who printed them. They were, in fact, produced on a secret press which was frequently moved from place to place to avoid detection. One of the men behind all these exceedingly ribald missives was Job Throckmorton, nephew of Clement of Haseley Manor.

The press travelled from Daventry to Coventry, thence to Wolston Priory, and from there to Haseley Manor, still churning out the scurrilous Marprelate Tracts. It was at Haseley Manor it was discovered. Two men, John Penry and John Udall were found with it, arrested and cast into prison. Penry was eventually hanged in 1593. It was never proved that Job Throckmorton actually wrote any of the tracts, and he escaped punishment, but it was thought at the time, and still is, that he escaped not because of lack of proof, but because of 'friends at Court'. His uncle Clement was a man of eminence and learning, and had served in sundry parliaments, so it is not unreasonable to expect him to have been able to 'pull strings'.

The old manor house remained with the Throckmorton family until 1725, and ultimately came into the hands of a Mr Alfred Hewlett who in Victorian times rebuilt it in the Tudor-Elizabethan style fashionable in his day.

Clement Throckmorton and his wife Katherine Nevill lie together in a large table top tomb in Haseley church, in a specially constructed bay of Kenilworth sandstone on the south side of the chancel. From the outside this rather grand bay looks like the window of a Tudor mansion, and not without cause, for it is said to have been built from the stones of the original manor house where Clement and Katherine lived. The brasses on the tomb are of considerable interest. They are palimpsest brasses, which means to say brasses which have already been used once on the reverse. They are of Flemish origin, and no one knows quite how they found their way to Haseley.

Haseley church, dedicated to St Mary, is worth seeking out. It is believed to be one of the smallest in Warwickshire. It has stained glass more than five centuries old, still retains the 17th and 18th century high box pews, and is one of the very few remaining churches where the lighting is still by the soft glow of candles. The font is of the 15th century and has roses carved upon four of its sides. In this font in 1620 was baptised Dr Annersley, the maternal grandfather of John and Charles Wesley.

A bit of 'hidden' Warwickshire came to the fore here in 1956 when necessary repairs meant that a certain portion of plaster had to be removed. Well hidden, behind this plaster, was a blocked-in Norman doorway, with the faint traces of painted biblical texts above it.

Also well hidden, and likely to remain so, is a wooden box containing every coin new minted in the year 1900. In this year the church porch was built, and the wooden box was buried in the great stone walls. This is perhaps a bit of Warwickshire that will remain hidden for another century or so.

Henley-in-Arden

Henley-in-Arden is justly famous for many things. Firstly it has what is probably one of the finest High Streets in the country. A mile long, it has so far managed to avoid any undesirable widening or straightening, despite the undoubted volume of traffic. Its buildings are of many styles and ages, all from the 15th century onwards, and yet all managing to nudge each other in perfect equanimity.

For its late building, it has to blame the de Montforts. All of Henley belonged to that family and just outside of the town is the little hill the locals call The Mount, all that remains of the castle of the de Montforts at Beaudesert, the adjoining hamlet. When Simon de Montfort was killed at the Battle of Evesham, Henley-in-Arden was burned to the ground. But it rose again quite rapidly, so that all its buildings are post-de Montfort.

The two churches, St John the Baptist's at Henley-in-Arden and St Nicholas' at Beaudesert, are separated by no more than a few hundred yards, and a tiny brook runs between. Beaudesert has a memorial tablet to Rev Richard Jago, father of the Warwickshire poet, also Richard Jago, who was born here. His poems, long out of fashion, are of the more lengthy, sycophantic and tedious kind.

Henley-in-Arden has a superb Guild Hall, a High Bailiff, ale tasters, brook lookers, butter weighers and beer tasters, together with quite a lot of pleasing civic ceremonial. There are many coaching inns, for this used to be the main route to London, and fortunately the inns have survived relatively unscathed. As one may imagine, most of them have ghosts.

One such ghost has recently been making quite a nuisance of herself at the White Swan in High Street, a venerable inn now owned by actor Michael Elphick. Guests have been disturbed by the ghost of a beautiful young woman in white, said to be about 5 ft 5 inches tall, with long auburn hair and sad pitiful eyes. A ghost researcher called in has declared it to be the wraith of 18 year old Virginia Black, daughter of a one-time host at the Swan. She, it seems, fell in love with Henry Becket, a farm labourer. They quarrelled upon the staircase on 23rd June 1845, and Henry pushed her so that she fell downstairs. Seeing the girl lying unmoving, Becket fled. Virginia recovered enough to drag herself back upstairs, and promptly expired upon the threshold of the room she haunts.

The poet William Shenstone was rather fond of the White

Swan too, and visited it many times. It is said that it was here, in about 1750, he wrote:

> Whoe'er has travelled life's dull round
> Where'er his journeys may have been
> Must sigh to think he still has found
> His warmest welcome at an inn.

One of Henley-in-Arden's most famous rogues was William Booth. The Booth family lived at Hall End Farm, just outside of Henley-in-Arden. They were farmers, and brothers John and William worked for their father. But in the latter half of the 18th century, farming was not all that prosperous, and it seemed to John and William they were working almost for nothing. Both wondered who would get the farm when the old man, their father, died.

William got fed up first, and left home to take on a farm of his own near to Birmingham. When Booth senior died, therefore, his eldest son, John inherited. William, apparently, didn't take kindly to this, and returned to Hall End to demand something for himself. The two brothers met in the stables and quarrelled violently. John was found dead with head injuries, and William was arrested and charged with his murder. The prosecution alleged William had picked up a shovel and attacked his brother. The defence said the injuries to John's head were caused by being kicked by a heavy farm horse. William declared himself innocent and said his brother had been alive when he left. He was believed, and allowed to go free.

Some four years or so later, William, now married and with two daughters, set himself up in the forgery business at his lonely and isolated farm. He had a couple of friends in his gang, and his wife assisted in the operation. It seems he did quite well, was well liked in the neighbourhood, gave to the poor, and was generally a 'good fellow'. But ultimately he was caught and arrested. Forgery was a capital offence in those days, and after his trial in 1812, William was sentenced to be hanged.

A large crowd gathered on the appointed day, and the march to the scaffold went according to plan. The hood was pulled down over the condemned man's head and the noose put around his neck, but when the lever was pulled, Booth just fell down because someone had neglected to fix the rope to the 'tree'. Although Booth was a bit bruised, he was still very much in the land of the living. A second time, he was put to stand upon the trap, the pre-arranged signal given, and again the trap failed. It was not until the third time that Booth was efficiently hanged, his last exit made.

As maybe imagined, all those watching read into this strange procedure a whole host of omens. They declared it was Booth's punishment for getting away with his brother's murder a few years before . It has to be said that Booth behaved with complete dignity throughout the entire farce. Booth might not have been a very adept criminal. Had he been, he would not have been caught quite so soon. But experts are united in declaring him to have been one of the best forgers the Midlands has ever produced.

Hillborough

➤ The 'Haunted Hillborough' of the famous jingle attributed to Shakespeare is isolated, romantic and mysterious. A place full of questions that are unlikely ever to find answer.

It is one of Warwickshire's lost villages and once had its own chapel dedicated to St Mary Magdalen, but this was pulled down in the 16th century by the lord of the manor, John Hubaud, who sold its bells and other ornaments for money.

There is scarce anything left, except a part of the old manor house basking comfortably in the sunlight at the end of a mile or so of twisty lane. Here lived Anne Whateley, whose name appears on a marriage licence issued on 27th November 1582 by the Bishop of Worcester to William Shakespeare. On the following day the same Bishop issued a bond enabling William to marry Anne Hathaway. Normally marriages did not take place during Advent, but Anne was three months pregnant at the time. There have been many theories put forward regarding Shakespeare's 'other Anne' and the most acceptable one seems to have been that he did court Anne Whateley, but at the same time Anne Hathaway, who was a servant girl in the manor at Hillborough, succumbed only too readily to the charms of the young 'well shaped' Will. Her family forced a quick marriage, and Anne Whateley was left alone.

Anne Whateley was the daughter of unmarried parents. Her father Captain Anthony Jenkinson was an ambassador to the court of Queen Elizabeth I, a minor poet and an adventurer. Her mother was Anne Beck, related to the Whateley family, and she died in childbirth. Anne Whateley eventually became a nun of the Order of St Clare, and wrote poetry under the name Ignoto (Unknown). A copy of *The Arte of English Poesie*, printed by Richard Field of Stratford-upon-Avon, is now in the British Museum. Anne is supposed to have quietly pined away after William left her, and is buried in the spot where Hillborough churchyard used to be, but is no longer.

At the top of the lane leading to Hillborough is the site of Shakespeare's 'crab'. This relates to the story of the Bidford Topers and the Stratford Sippers. It seems that Bidford prided itself very highly on being able to quaff ale in large quantities. So much so that they regularly invited teams from surrounding villages to see if they could beat them at it.

One such team was the Stratford Sippers, among whom was William Shakespeare. The contest was at the Falcon Inn, Bidford, and accordingly the Stratford team turned up. Many times were the ale pots filled, and many times emptied, but once again the Bidford Topers won. The Stratford team were beaten, and were eventually taken from the Falcon and set on the right road to home, seven miles off.

They didn't quite make it. Or at least some of them didn't. They fell into a drunken torpor beneath a crab apple tree on the side of the road, near to Hillborough. Shakespeare awoke in the morning, so it is said, and composed the rhyme:

> Piping Pebworth, Dancing Marston,
> Haunted Hillborough and Hungry Grafton
> With Dodging Exhall, Papist Wixford
> Beggarly Broom and Drunken Bidford.

These surrounding villages are all included because they had teams of ale quaffers, and with such a thick head, he thought he must have been drinking against them all. Except, that is, - Haunted Hillborough. No one quite knows why he included this one, except that for him it is likely Hillborough would always be haunted.

The venerable crab, marked on Ordnance sheets as Shakespeare's Crab in the past, went to its final home in 1824, its demise hastened by being hacked about for souvenirs. It has been replaced, but naturally it doesn't have the same feel about it, and it is no longer marked on maps.

Haunted, though, Hillborough most certainly is! One such ghost is the Screaming Man, said to be the wicked landlord who turned peasants off their land so that he might raise the more lucrative sheep. One night they gathered themselves together and attacked his house, causing much damage and terrifying him so much that he screamed. And has been regularly screaming ever since.

One of the fields down the Hillborough lane is still known as Palmer's Piece, and thereby hangs (literally) another tale. John Palmer was a murderer. Together with his mother and his sister Hannah, he brutally murdered his wife by cutting her throat in November 1800. The callous trio then threw the poor woman's body into the river Avon, not far from Hillborough.

That particular November, the Avon burst its banks, and when the waters eventually subsided, the body of John Palmer's wife was found, lodged in a weir brake. Palmer, his mother and sister were arrested and thrown into Warwick gaol. The mother never came to trial but died in her cell, never having once shown the slightest sign of remorse. The brother and sister were tried, found guilty and sentenced to be hanged. John Palmer's body was to be hung in chains on the land now known as Palmer's Piece, as near as possible to where his wife's murdered body was discovered. Hannah Palmer's body was given to the Stratford-upon-Avon surgeon to be dissected.

Both bodies were brought from Warwick in a cart on a broiling hot Good Friday in 1801, and the sentence of the court complied with. The doctor couldn't be bothered overmuch with Hannah at the time, and her body lay in his garden for several days before he could get round to dealing with it. Palmer's body hung in chains on Palmer's Piece until it rotted and fell. But not before one good dame in Hillborough had taken for herself a piece of his finger bone. The bone of a hanged felon is said to have curative properties, and this lady kept the gruesome relic in her workbox to the end of her life. Her great nephew, F. W. Bennett tells the story in his *Tiddyoody Pie* (1930).

Needless to say, Palmer hasn't gone anywhere. His shade, probably still entirely without remorse, may be seen flitting across the Piece. Just as Anne Whateley is said not to have left the manor, but gentle, beautiful and radiant, has been seen gliding gracefully through walls and doors, the 'White Lady of Hillborough.

Honiley

Here in this wild and isolated spot, once tucked away in the ancient Forest of Arden, Simon de Montfort, Earl of Leicester, built himself a house and made it his home. Perhaps he had become tired of soldiering and of perpetual battlefields, for he obtained a licence from the Pope to build a church here and to put within the church a statue dedicated to St John and a picture of the Blessed Virgin.

He arranged that the church should have enough money by giving the Abbot of Kenilworth some of the lands in his possession, and asked that masses be said twice a year for his immortal soul and the souls of his successors. The monks of Kenilworth were to pay a nominal rent of one sparrow-hawk, payable on St James's Day, for all the lands given to them by de Montfort.

Many pilgrims flocked to Honiley, for its fame spread across the country, and not just because de Montfort had built a church here. Two wells had been discovered within the vicinity of the newly built church. One was called St John's Well after the patron saint of the church, the other was called Our Lady's Well. These were used for a very special purpose.

It was said that all those men who lived a 'lewd life' and had gotten a maiden with chylde' must make pilgrimage to St John's Well if they were to save their immortal souls. They must bathe and wash themselves within this well, and ask pardon for the heavy weight of their sins. This being completed, they must enter the church, and upon their knees crawl towards the figure of St John. There, the priest would give them absolution and a small bottle of the healing water of St John's Well, provided, of course, they had the necessary coins with which to pay the fine the church levied upon them.

The women, having been delivered of their child 'gotten upon them' must make their way to Our Lady's Well, accompanied by the midwife who attended the confinement. There they too must publicly bathe their sins away, and enter the church upon their knees, crawling towards the picture of the Virgin, where once again, with suitable payment of fines, they would be given absolution and a bottle of the healing water. Many and numerous were the pilgrims treading the paths to these holy wells, and they certainly kept the priests busy. Sometimes it ended happily, with the priest convincing the two people concerned to enter into marriage, but alas more often than not the 'guilty' couple went their separate ways.

Despite de Montfort's building of the church to heal the wounds of so many battles fought upon this land, there was still to be another bloody skirmish, for it was here in July 1469, during the Wars of the Roses, that King Edward IV was captured by Richard Neville, Earl of Warwick – Warwick the Kingmaker – and taken to his great castle in the county town.

The church of St John still dominates the landscape at Honiley, but it is not the church of Simon de Montfort. Honiley was purchased by John Saunders, who became lord of the manor and built himself a grand Hall. The outbuildings still remain, converted to modern houses, but the old Hall was pulled down round about 1820. You may still see traces of the Saunders coat of arms, which includes elephant heads, upon some of the gates. A new Hall was built in 1914, and this now belongs to the

County Council who use it for educational purposes. Apart from this Hall, the converted outbuildings and the church, there is little else to Honiley.

But to return to John Saunders. He decided, having built himself a Hall, he would like to rebuild the church. Such an undertaking is not to be taken lightly, but Saunders was fortunate in having as his near neighbour Sir Christopher Wren, whose son lived at nearby Wroxall Abbey. Saunders invited Sir Christopher to dine with him; not an unusual occurrence, since the two men had become friends. 'I want to rebuild the church', said Saunders to his guest. Whereupon, according to legend at any rate, Sir Christopher rapidly sketched a rough design upon the white tablecloth spread across the dining table! Wren was an old man by this time, nearing his 90th birthday. He died that same year, 1723.

Saunders went ahead with his plan to rebuild the church of St John. As apparently no one thought to preserve this historic tablecloth, no one will ever know whether or not Wren's design was acted upon. The church is unmistakably baroque, and very beautiful, but experts now seem to think that whether or not Wren put the idea into Saunders' head, the work is more likely to have been executed by the local and notable architect, Francis Smith of Warwick.

Honington

One of the most graceful villages in the whole of Warwickshire, Honington is approached off the main A34 Shipston-on-Stour road through two ornamental gate pillars surmounted by decorative stone 'pineapples', thus giving the impression of entering on to a private estate. Indeed, gates used to hang upon these pillars, and the road to the village was once a private one, winding through well wooded park land up to the gates of Honington Hall.

The village has wide neatly trimmed greens and truly lovely old houses, ranging from a tea-cosy thatched cottage to a long and low brick and timber. All is so carefully preserved as to look almost unreal. All is beautiful in Honington, and yet within its church is what has been described as the 'ugliest cherub' in the whole country.

Like so many other villages it used once to belong to a religious house, which in 1257 managed to get the King's blessing for a rather odd system of work and payment for services performed by their serfs and villeins. These men had to be available to mow, harrow, cart and move hay between the Feast of St John and Michaelmas, and for their labour were to receive a 'mutton', eight loaves and a cheese.

At the Dissolution of the Monasteries, the estate was sold to the Gybbes family, who ultimately disposed of it to Sir Henry Parker, a rich London merchant. He promptly built himself a grand house in 1682. Some experts describe Honington Hall as a fine classical specimen, others have declared it to be 'finnicky'. It obviously was intended to be fashionable, and to show the world that Henry Parker was a rich man. It has some rococo work which is thought to be by Charles Stanley, the Anglo-Danish craftsman who lived in England for 20 years, 1726-1746, and was much employed.

Sir Henry Parker, his mansion almost complete, turned his attention to the church. Again it is rebuilt in the classical style, and is often referred to as a 'Wren-style' church. The lower part of the 13th century tower was allowed to remain.

Sir Henry Parker has the most imposing monument inside the small church, dominating one wall. Massive in marble, Sir Henry is shown more than life size, standing chatting to his son Hugh, who died before him. Both men are plump, well dressed, be-laced and be-wigged, and beneath their feet are three columns in Latin extolling the early virtues they each possessed. Close by is a plain slab to Dame Ann Parker, wife of Sir Henry Parker, who died in 1731 at the age of 19, and two of her daughters who lived to be 54 years and 83 years respectively.

After the Parkers came the Townsends, and it is the memorial to Joseph Townsend that visitors come to see. It is an excellent piece of work, although somewhat nightmarish in its conception. There is the skull symbolic of mortality, but the cherub is positively evil, with a squeezed, elongated misshapen head and the most malevolent expression. There are a couple of Westmacott memorials to later Townsends.

The Townsend family lived for a long time at Honington Hall, and it was in 1875 that Mrs Mary Elizabeth Townsend started the Girls Friendly Society here, with meetings held in her home. From this small beginning, the work of the Society rapidly spread across the country, providing activities and friendship for young girls in villages, towns and cities. Quite soon, the Hall meetings moved to Shipston-on-Stour, and the Townsend family gave a piece of land in the middle of the town for the building of a hall which is still much used and is still called the Townsend Hall.

One of the delights of Honington is the small 17th century bridge over the river Stour, its decorative stonework topped by some 22 stone balls. The bridge has to be negotiated, and sadly there are times when for the motorist this is not a successful manoeuvre. Its hump and curve can be misjudged, and when this happens it usually ends up with a stone ball or two plopping into the Stour beneath. Replacement of these stone balls over the years has been a costly business. Shipston-on-Stour sub-aqua club recently decided to do a few dives beneath the bridge, and managed to resurrect several stone balls capable of re-use.

Hunningham

Very well hidden in this tiny hamlet, to the west of the great straight Fosse Way, and the 'ham of Hunna's people' at the time of the Domesday survey. It stands by the river Leam, in pleasant although not outstanding broad countryside, and is a mixture of old small cottages and new houses. The school, provided to accommodate the numerous progeny of farm labourers, once doubtless rang to the cries of children who, in the way of all children, would probably have preferred to be running wild in the fields instead of sitting in the Victorian classroom. It is now converted to a private house.

The Leam is crossed by a bridge of massive arches, dating from medieval times and then refurbished in the 17th century when villagers were forever having to contend with flooding problems. It has recently been the object of further attention, and still remains a most impressive bridge.

The tiny church of St Margaret is ancient, and was completed in the 13th century by the family of Corbucion, who owned this manor. Very few churches anywhere managed to escape the hand of the Victorian restorer, but in this case it rested but lightly. The lichen-covered tiled roof has a boarded bell turret, and within is a memorial to a young man of a very strange name. It seems Hannibel Horseye died at the age of 25 years in 1623, but who he was and how he came by such an extraordinary appellation is not known.

Hunningham's history has been fairly uneventful, but it did achieve a certain amount of unwelcome notoriety in the 19th century when it housed a pauper lunatic asylum. Mr James Thomas Harcourt was an official at the Warwick Union Workhouse, and doubtless with his eye to a good thing as far as profit goes, he left his job and started a private asylum at Hunningham House in 1846. He was licensed to house 78 pauper lunatics, and took the worst cases from the workhouse, for which he was paid a fee per person. This was obviously cheaper than the overcrowded workhouse attempting to house them.

In 1849 Dr Alfred Carr, the medical man attending at Hunningham House, laid an official complaint against Harcourt and his establishment by writing to the Commissioners in Lunacy and calling for an enquiry. He alleged that the inmates had been regularly beaten with whips, ill treated, forced into solitary confinement in a brick cell where they were kept naked without even a blanket, forced to sit beneath cold showers, and any belongings, however pitiful they might be, removed from them.

According to Dr Carr, these poor souls were treated in a most inhumane and cruel way, regarded with no compassion at all. Even when the doctor declared they were fit to be released, Harcourt had refused to release them, thinking that in doing so he would be losing his fee.

Several of the local labourers and their wives gave evidence of seeing the inmates beaten, being dragged back to Hunningham House by their hair, laid about with stout cudgels and so forth. But despite all this, the Commissioners decided there was no case to answer and Harcourt was rendering a valuable service to the community by housing these unfortunates. Despite Dr Carr's careful notes, nothing at all was done about Hunningham House.

In this small peaceful hamlet, the goings-on at the lunatic asylum caused a great deal of worry. One elderly lady was frightened when returning home after dark to see all the lunatics disporting themselves in the churchyard by playing leapfrog over the gravestones. The good dame presumably thought the dead had suddenly risen to confront her!

By 1850 Hunningham House had closed down, presumably because the profit had gone out of pauper lunacy. Harcourt emigrated to Australia, where he founded the very first private madhouse in the State of Victoria.

Hunningham House settled down into private ownership, and Hunningham itself soon forgot the unfortunates who had been with them for five years.

Idlicote

This village certainly comes into the category of 'hidden' Warwickshire, for well secluded it is, and even smaller than before. It now houses no more than 70 souls, whereas in the past the population has risen to somewhere around 100.

Warwickshire villages are often set forth in couplets, and apart from the famous one about 'drunken Bidford' attributed to our most famous son, Shakespeare, there is yet another one along the same lines:

> Idlicote on the hill, Whatcote downderry
> Beggardly Oxhill, lousy Fulready
> Yawning Yettington (Ettington),
> Peeping Pillardington (Pillerton)
> And one-eyed Marston.

Tho whom this can be attributed, or even exactly what it means, no one can tell, but it is often quoted.

Idlicote is certainly 'on the hill' and clusters around a large and rather pretty pond. The school has been converted to a house, and nearby is a small group of houses which must have once housed the children attending the small school.

The estate belonged to the monks of Kenilworth until Henry VIII dissolved all the religious houses and gave Idlicote to Thomas Cawarden, his Master of the Revels, whose job it was to devise entertainments for this not-so-easily pleased monarch. Queen Elizabeth I stayed here on one of her many progresses through Warwickshire, and when Cawarden died without an heir, she granted the estate to the wicked 'Loddy' Greville, who ultimately was 'pressed to death' for the murder of his servant. But before he committed this dreadful deed, he sold Idlicote to William Underhill. The Underhills were one of the foremost families of Warwickshire, and indeed so prolific were they, they had houses, seats and heirs in almost every village in the south of the county. This William Underhill acquired the estate in 1567. He was also the owner of a much better known property – New Place, Stratford-Upon-Avon, which he sold to William Shakespeare.

William Underhill, alas, came to a fearful end. He had married his cousin, Mary Underhill from nearby Ettington. They were first cousins on both sides, and this may have accounted for the strange nature of their first child, a son named Fulke, who was constantly involved in some litigation or other, and was definitely the black sheep of the clan. At the age of just 18, so anxious was he to claim his inheritance and to acquire power, that he got tired of waiting for it and murdered his father by poison on 7th July 1597. He was tried for his crime and hanged at Warwick in March of the following year, when the great bell of St Nicholas in that town tolled for his untimely passing.

His brother Hercules Underhill paid the necessary fine to recover his estates from the Crown, who had seized them as belong to a felon. The Idlicote branch adhered to the Old Faith and the wife of Sir Hercules, the Lady Bridget, was fined 1s 4d for recusancy in 1628. The Ettington Underhills on the other hand were Puritans, and in the Civil War espoused the side Parliament, whereas Sir Hercules and the Idlicote branch followed the King. This led to some estrangement, but it was short lived.

They seem to have been rather a hot-headed lot, however, for in the reign of Charles II, Sir William Underhill of Idlicote was fined £1,500 for wounding a man called Devereaux with a pistol, and when Sir William refused to pay such a heavy fine, his Idlicote house and lands were confiscated. But Sir William gathered together a party of strong-minded men, and together they forced entry into Idlicote House, ejecting Devereaux and his men, and in the process killing one of them. And they appear to have got away with it!

The Underhill connection at Idlicote ended about 1755, and later the old manor house was largely rebuilt by Sir John Soane. Portions of the old moat still remained until fairly recently, and there are tales of subterranean passages through the cellars. Presumably all ready for a quick get-away should such become necessary. These are, of course, from the much older house which stood upon the site, and not the present one.

The old house has seen many changes as the centuries have rolled over its benign head. In the 19th century it was the home of the Peach and the Peach Keighley family, some members of which died in the service of the East India Company, wherein the foundations of their fortune were laid. They are buried here, and have memorials.

In 1900 Lord Southampton made Idlicote House his home, and during the Second World War it was turned into billets for members of the Women's Land Army, whose sterling work was so much needed on the surrounding farms. Many of them didn't go back, but married locals and stayed with us.

The church is a collector's gem with its large box pew for the family of the 'big house', and an unusual three decker pulpit with tester, thought to be the only one of its kind in Warwickshire.

Near to the church is a large stone tower, originally the dovecote moved from Kenilworth by the monks of the abbey there, and doubtless used at Idlicote to provide meat for the holy brothers.

90

Ilmington

Ilmington must be one of the loveliest villages in all Warwickshire, with old stone, mullion-windowed houses, lanes leading nowhere, small brooks meandering, and a backcloth of the softly undulating Cotswolds.

High up on Ilmington Downs, the highest point within the county, you may look down the slopes to glimpse the old manor house of Lark Stoke, and the field nearby is called locally 'the town' because from humps, hollows and expert opinion, it would seem there was once much more of a settlement here than just the only manor house, lovely though it is.

In 1433, a man called Edward Dauntsey was living in an old house on this spot, but we know little of him. Shortly after this, George Colchester was the owner and resident, and George Colchester had a daughter, Margery, his only child and heir to his lands.

To Lark Stoke in the year 1487, when the Wars of the Roses were still rumbling on, came a man calling himself John Buston from Somerset. It is generally believed that he was some kind of fugitive from the aftermath of those troublesome times. No one knows why he came to Lark Stoke, unless he was on his way to somewhere much more important and, deciding there could be nowhere in England more pleasant, settled himself here.

He fell in love with Margery Colchester, disclosed that his real name was Brent, and they were married. They founded a whole dynasty of Brents of Lark Stoke, and in many parish records they are known as 'Brent alias Buston' for it seems it took a long time for John Buston to assume his true identity.

The family were at Lark Stoke until 1768. By that time there were only four sisters, three named Brent, and one Dame Elizabeth Lytcot, a widow. The four ladies lived in straightened circumstances, letting out their bits of land. They were listed as non-jurors and papists, and the ultimate survivor was Dame Lytcot. She is buried, with the Brent forbears, in Ilmington church. She seems to have been a formidable and somewhat lonely old lady, always known as 'Madam', and she seems to have died virtually penniless, for the sexton records no funeral expenses for her, and all she left was a box of books of Catholic devotions. She is perhaps best remembered for the fact that she had three pear trees, with rather a strange taste to the fruit. She was rather jealous of the trees, and indeed their fruit was not to everyone's liking. No one knows what variety they were, and they were always referred to simply as 'Madam's' pears. Grafts of this fruit grew in many corners of Ilmington, and were still enjoyed earlier this century.

Lark Stoke was taken over after the Brents by John Hart of Shipston-on-Stour. He was a wealthy man, a weaver of shag and plush, and more or less unaided brought a degree of prosperity to the area. However, the worthy Mr Hart must have been greatly distressed when after his death his heirs did nothing but quarrel among themselves over their inheritance, and went to law about it so often that the wealth he had amassed through skill and acumen was completely dissipated paying for all the litigation. Lark Stoke was taken over by the Court of Chancery and sold to the Corbetts. There is a strange stone to one Hutton Corbett, just outside the church door, which tells us he lived to the ripe old age of 106 years, nine months and eleven days!

There is a little bit of hidden 'Yorkshire' within the church, if you care to search. The beautiful oak wood work is by Thompsons of Kilburn, Yorkshire. Thompson used a rather special signature; a tiny carving of a church mouse, and there are eleven such signatures within the church, all well hidden, but there if you look.

Kings Newnham

A turning off the Fosse Way, towards the eastern part of the county, brings you to the tiny hamlet of Kings Newnham, so small and secluded that should you blink, you will have passed through it altogether, and this would be a pity for Kings Newnham has a ghostly beauty all of its own.

Had Lady Luck been less fickle, Kings Newnham might have become a spa on the same level as Bath, Cheltenham or

Leamington. For here in 1579 a chalybeate spring was discovered, quite by chance, by a farm worker called Clement Dawes.

It seems that Dawes was about his daily work when carelessly he injured his arm with a hatchet, causing a severe wound from which the blood gushed forth. His first instinct was to get water and accordingly he headed towards this spring in the fields, and immersed the injured arm. Not only did he find relief from the pain, the arm healed up as good as new within a couple of days, and it was realised that the spring water had healing properties.

Dawes became something of a celebrity and in 1582 Walter de Bailey, physician to Queen Elizabeth I declared the spring to be beneficial and recommended its waters to all and sundry. There was some local attempt to build a well house above the spring, and much later its reputation came to the ears of Queen Anne who visited it herself. However, either the idea didn't quite catch on, or there was no one around at the time with sufficient foresight and finance to develop it. The well house fell into disrepair. In 1857 more work was done on the well house, but by that time nearby Leamington Spa had become the fashionable watering place in the area, and Kings Newnham's chalybeate spring lapsed back into happy obscurity.

The building that dominates Kings Newnham is the tower of the old church of St Lawrence, leaning lopsided and still showing traces of Norman work. What was once the nave now forms part of a farmyard wall, and the Hall of the old Newnham Regis standing close by is now a farm, the farmyard being formed from the old graveyard of the church.

The Hall used to be the home of Lord John Scott, son of the Duke of Buccleuch, kinsman of the Leigh family of Stoneleigh Abbey. One day, sometime during the 1850s, Lord John held a shooting party at Kings Newnham. There was much sport, but this was later dampened by a torrential shower of rain and the party hurried from the woodland back to the Hall for lunch. They struggled across the farmyard which was already ankle deep in muddy water, and one of the party irritably declared

St Lawrence's church tower at Kings Newnham

that it was the way of all farmyards to turn themselves into a muddy swamp at the first drop of rain.

After a light lunch, it was noticed the rain had stopped and the party once more made their way outdoors. They were quite astonished to find the farmyard almost dried out and all the water disappeared. The irritable man became curious, and taking up a stick, began to poke around trying to discover where all the water had drained away so rapidly. He found a small hole, poked it a bit, made it bigger, and found himself staring down into a rain filled vault! As he looked a lead coffin came floating towards him. He pushed it away with his stick, but it was rapidly followed by others.

The party, mystified, called in the local blacksmith and had the lead rolled back off the coffins. One was found to contain the body of Francis, Earl of Chichester and Lord Dunsmore, buried in 1653; in another the body of Sir John Anderson, the son of Lady Chichester by her first husband; in Lady Chichester's coffin, they found nothing but a skeleton, and an abundance of thick glossy auburn hair.

In the coffin of Lady Audrey Leigh, wife of Francis, Earl of Chichester, they found the body in perfect condition, though she had been buried in 1640. It seems the lady had been young and very beautiful. They said she looked no more than 16. Her flesh was plump and rosy, her eyebrows and eyelashes made perfect curves, and her tiny hands were folded across her fine linen, trimmed all over with five-point lace. In her tiny ears were rings in the shape of black enamelled serpents.

But the last coffin was the strangest of all. When it was opened, the air was filled with a pungent and aromatic scent. Inside the coffin was the body of a handsome man, beautifully embalmed, with leaves of rosemary and other herbs completely covering him. He had a peaked beard and a quantity of long brown hair, somewhat spotted with blood around the neck, and no wonder, for he had been beheaded. His head had been put back upon his neck and tied around with black velvet ribbon. His hands were folded peacefully upon his breast and, embroidered upon the fine linen he wore, were the initials 'T.B.'

worked in black silk. Lord John Scott had the coffins repaired and properly and reverently buried, with a zinc cover and brass tomb plate to keep the vault dry. But the mystery remained. Who was the beheaded man?

No one can ever know for certain, because during the early part of the 19th century there was one of those interminable law suits about succession in the Leigh family. It was during this period that someone cut from the parish registers all the entries relating to the Leighs and their time at Kings Newnham. The culprit was never discovered.

It is, however, known that the Leighs were Royalists, and two of them, Thomas and John Brierley of Lancaster, were officers in the King's Army during the Civil War. Faced with capture or defeat, they fled and headed towards Kings Newnham, home of their kinsmen. John went to earth and survived, but Thomas was captured, and the family believed he was executed. Could he be the unknown that lies buried beneath the ancient tower at Kings Newnham? The dates and the initials would fit. But who was it then that reclaimed his mutilated body and so carefully prepared it for honourable and secret burial? The young man suffered greatly for his allegiance to his King. Perhaps he now finds peace beneath this ghostly tower, dose to his kin and the lovely Lady Audrey.

Kinwarton

➤ Tucked right away down a fairly obscure side lane, well rutted, the intrepid voyager will discover Kinwarton's main claim to fame these days: a 14th century dovecote which used once to provide meat for the Abbot of Evesham. The building now belongs to the National Trust and is marked upon their literature, but unless you know where to look you'll have a job finding it!

Kinwarton was given to the Abbey of Evesham by King Cenred of Mercia in AD708, and the remains of the old manor house, called by the monks Kinwarton Grange, may still be seen together with the banks of the former ponds used to provide the Friday meal of fish.

The dovecote is said to be one of the very earliest of its kind, and its very small entrance has an ogee arch, typical of the 14th century. It is of circular plan, and the lantern light above was added some three centuries later.

Once inside, and eyes accustomed to the gloom, it is quite astonishing. The walls are some three feet thick and contain 500 nesting holes. There is a vertical beam in the centre, with a pivot top and bottom. From this beam, called properly a 'potence', horizontal beams project to support a ladder which can thus be pushed around the whole circumference with ease. The monk in charge of the birds would be able to reach into all of the 500 nests.

Pigeon meat was a much prized addition to the abbot's table, and if history tells us aright, abbots liked to dine well. They were also required to feed and offer shelter to travellers so a self-

Kinwarton dovecote

perpetuating supply of some 500 birds would prove very useful.

The church held this manor for 832 years, until the Dissolution of the Monasteries when it passed into the hands of the Skinner family, who made their money in London. Since the dovecote continued in use, it is assumed that the Skinners also enjoyed pigeon meat. The old house was destroyed sometime before 1754, by which time it was being used as a farm house.

As one may expect in a hamlet with ecclesiastical origins, there is a beautiful old church, standing within a stone's throw of the dovecote. The church of St Mary is surrounded by trees, with a splendid view of the open Alne countryside. It was rebuilt in 1316 on the site of a much earlier and probably less permanent structure.

One of the most interesting items within the church is an alabaster 'table' or panel, presented by the two Miss Purtons of Alcester in memory of their grandfather and great-grandfather. It shows the dedication of the Madonna, Joachim and Anne bringing Mary to the Temple, with five veiled women standing, and a priest with an angel at his feet. Dating from the 15th century, it is thought to have once been part of a more important reredos, but from whence it originated no one seems to have been able to find out.

The great-grandfather of the Miss Purtons was Francis Rufford, rector of Kinwarton from 1787 until his death in 1833, some 46 years. He it was who built the rectory near to the church, now a private house. One of his sons, William, became rector of Binton just a few miles off, from 1820 until 1836, and this William was grandfather to the Miss Purtons. It was William who discovered the alabaster panel.

It seems he was visiting the local village carpenter in Binton, and finding the workshop interesting began poking about a bit, as one does! Beneath a pile of shavings and sawdust in a corner, he came upon this treasure. He questioned the carpenter who replied, in effect, 'Oh, that old thing. That's been lying around in here for years; ever since my father's time and probably before that. You can have it if you want it'. Whereupon Rev William thought he had better take it into safe custody.

The Miss Purtons were also descendants of Dr Thomas Purton (1768-1833) who lived in Alcester. Purton was a dedicated botanist, and his work *Midland Flora* still remains a veritable bible for those working in this field. The Purtons and the Ruffords were connected by marriage and are buried at Kinwarton, including the grandson of the noted Dr Thomas, Henry Bloxam Purton, who also served as rector of Kinwarton.

The incumbents at Kinwarton appear to have been somewhat concerned about where and how they should be buried. Leonard Clarke who died in 1662 left instructions that he was to be buried between his two wives 'yet as near to the body of my last wife as may conveniently be. . . '.

William Edes instructed he must be buried in the chancel of Kinwarton church, on the south side and within the communion rails. 'I would have all the neighbours at Kinwarton both rich and poor to be invited to my funeral, all my tenants. Every poor family at Kinwarton to receive 12d', he says. There is no trace of his burial within the church. His servant Isaac Dipple made a will in 1729, and he also wished to have all the neighbours of Kinwarton attend his funeral and wished to be buried in the chancel 'as nigh my late master as possible'.

Langley

Langley is really only a small lane; one of those very typical of Warwickshire at its old-fashioned leafiest, narrow, twisting, with great high banks topped with hedges upon either side. As you head downwards towards Langley you get ample warning of floods, for in times of heavy rainfall Langley becomes even more isolated and as the notice says, if you can see water, the road is impassable.

The old part of this very tiny hamlet has pretty black and white cottages, and they have sat basking in the sun for centuries. Things might well have continued thus except that after the Second World War, in the veritable explosion of development, Langley had new houses built for the first time in donkey's years.

Langley was a place of some minor importance in medieval times, for in the 12th century the monks of Saumur in France had a chapel in the village. Edward de Hereforde, owner of the manor, was allowed to fortify it sometime around 1340 and presumably he did so, but all trace has long since disappeared.

In the troublesome times of King John there was a long running dispute at Langley over the tithes, for the vicar of Wootton Wawen said he ought to have them and the rector of Claverdon was collecting them for himself. Everybody argued for years and years, and eventually the rector of Claverdon had to give the vicar of Wootton Wawen a pound of incense every year. No one knew what the final outcome of it all was, and probably by that time few really cared anyway.

One of the most astonishing events in tiny Langley over the last century was the setting up of the Old Swan Foundry, a country foundry started by William Troth in 1850 and run by his descendants right through until its closure in 1965.

William Troth came from the adjoining parish of Norton Lindsey, and used to work at the big house near Wootton Wawen, Edstone Hall. While he was doing this he set himself up in a small way as an agricultural implement maker, concentrating upon the traditional Warwickshire plough.

He did well. Warwickshire soil needed something special and by 1854 William Troth was all neatly set up in his own little foundry at Langley, making composite cast iron and wooden ploughs, cheap to buy, cheap to maintain, and the cast iron bits easily replaceable. He designed and made his own threshing machine, and he made an 'improved drawbar' which would enable three horses to plough abreast without trampling the ground already ploughed.

He built himself a cast iron cart, with cast iron hubs and wrought iron spokes and rims, all designed to advertise his skills, his foundry and his speciality, the single furrow horse-drawn plough. The cart, his trademark and recognisable for miles around, earned for him the nickname 'The Iron Duke'.

The foundry prospered, and as a further advertising venture 14 employees formed the Langley Ploughman's Brass Band, much in demand and thought to be very good.

In 1886 the firm merged with the Stratford firm of William Francis, who worked at the Old Swan Yard. The iron foundry was then centred upon Stratford-upon-Avon, while the plough making remained at Langley. Francis himself was a bit of an eccentric, not unlike Troth. Francis made for himself a superb cast iron coffin which during his lifetime stood upright against the wall and did duty as a cupboard.

Eventually, as the tractor took over, the firm of Troth lost business until in 1965 it closed. The patterns, tools and castings are now in the keeping of the Warwickshire County Museum, an integral part of the development of agriculture within the county, and the Iron Duke's firm is no more.

Little Compton

To this small, secluded village falls the distinction of being the southernmost within the county of Warwickshire. It is a peaceful and quiet place, for only a small signpost upon the main road tells you of its existence, down quiet lanes bordered by mature trees. The village green remains, and there are still working farms and an inn. And it has a manor house, one of the loveliest in all England I should think, where once lived a man who had looked upon a national tragedy of great enormity.

The manor house and the little church of St Denys blend into each other, both constructed of the local mellow, yellowish-grey stone that merges so well into the backdrop of the wolds. Inside the church is a memorial window to King Charles I, beheaded at Whitehall on 30th January 1649. It illustrates episodes in the tragedy; his walk in the snow, his farewells to his children, his ordeal on the scaffold, and his coffin carried into the chapel. What, you might ask, has the martyred King to do with the remote hamlet of Little Compton? Then upon the floor of the church you might spot a memorial slab bearing the name 'Juxon' and all is made clear.

Bishop William Juxon lived in this manor house. Friend and confidante of the King, he remained with him in his last days and accompanied him on to the dreadful scaffold set up in public outside the Palace of Whitehall. Bishop Juxon, heartbroken, grieving, watched as the King made his last farewells to his children. Juxon was despairing in his grief, so much so that the King turned to him and said gently, 'Leave all this my Lord. We have no more time for it . . '.

When he stood upon the scaffold, the King once more turned to his greatest and truest friend, Juxon, and told him to grieve no more, for 'I go from a corruptible to an incorruptible where no disturbance can be . . '. He then instructed Juxon to give his Garter Jewel, the 'George', to his sons with instructions that they were to forgive their father's murderers.

He gave Bishop Juxon the ring from his finger with one last word to him, his last word in this life, 'Remember'. And he then laid his head upon the block. William Juxon watched as the axe swished through the air and severed the head of his master from his slight body.

What of Juxon then? Strangely he suffered no harm at Cromwell's hands. He was robbed of his clerical offices and forbidden to say the offices of his Church, but he was allowed to come to live at Little Compton manor house, which he had inherited from his brother.

Here he lived the quiet life of a country gentleman. He diverted himself with a pack of hounds which 'exceeded all other hounds in England for the pleasure and orderly hunting of them . . .'. Cromwell knew of it; indeed kept an eye upon Juxon, but did not interfere. Perhaps he thought he had already done enough. Juxon, forbidden the church, used to repair to Chastleton, just over the border in Oxfordshire, a house of strong Royalist sympathies, and here he would say the mass in secret. He also gave into the keeping of this great house the bible the King had taken with him to his death.

Juxon survived to see the end of Cromwell the end of the Commonwealth, and the restoration of the monarchy. With the entry of Charles II into London, William Juxon gladly came out of retirement, and was made Archbishop of Canterbury. He died in 1663, at the age of 81.

Also commemorated at Little Compton is its patron saint, St Denys, who was also beheaded, although in his case it was at

Montmartre. The association stems from the fact that Little Compton used to belong to the Priory of Deerhurst in Gloucestershire, and Deerhurst was linked with the Abbey of St Denys in Paris. The windows to the saint and to the martyred king were given by Mrs Gertrude Leverton, who was fortunate enough to live in the old manor house from 1927 to 1938.

The manor house is no longer a private home, but the headquarters of a business college. It is said that occasionally the voice of Bishop William Juxon may be heard, in the quiet of the night, saying the offices of his Church that were denied to him for the eleven years he lived here.

Long Compton

It would not be strictly true to call this village hidden, for the busy main A34 passes straight through it, dispelling the romantic notion of sun-warmed stone and utter tranquillity.

It is a long village, curving gently on the edge of the Cotswolds, with fine old stone houses of varying periods on both sides of the road and many little offshoots of narrow lanes leading to other good houses in quiet backwaters. It has a superb old church with an unusual lychgate which has a room perched above it. This was at one time a cottage, built around the year 1600. The lower storey was removed and the whole made good, so that the visitor passes beneath the upper room to enter the churchyard.

But what Long Compton is really known for is witches! As the main road makes its way south, it ascends Long Compton Hill towards the Oxfordshire border. At the top of the hill stand the Rollright Stones, an ancient circle of dolmen. Legend has it these were once human, a king, his knights and followers. This king came marching up from the south and at the top of Long Compton Hill he met a witch who, with all the craft of her kind, knew him for an ambitious man. She told him to take seven strides to the top of the hill and:

> If Long Compton thou canst see
> King of England shalt thou be.

The Rollright Stones near Long Compton

He thought he had it made, and strode to the top of the hill confidently expecting to see Long Compton nestling below him. What the witch knew, and he did not, was that a spur or knob of land obscures the view of Long Compton from this point. The witch gave one of those cackles that only witches know how to make, and promptly turned the king and all the rest into stone.

The King Stone stands on one side of the road; on the opposite side is the stone circle, thought to be his followers, and a little way beyond them stand the Whispering Knights, thought to be the traitors who plotted together against this king. It is said that if a maiden of Long Compton should visit the Whispering Knights at dusk, at the time of the barley harvest, they will tell her if her love be true or not!

Not far from the Rollright Stones is a ford which crosses a narrow lane. This has been known as Traitors Ford since time immemorial, yet the origin of the name has never been found. Some people believe that it is called after those traitors turned into stone, the Whispering Knights.

This ancient stone circle is awash with legend; it is a place of atmosphere, going right back to long before the days of Arthur. Perhaps it is still used by witches celebrating their sabbat. It was in 1875 that the whole question of the witches of Long Compton came to light, when a frail 80 year old woman was discovered murdered with a pitchfork. A young man by the name of James Heywood was arrested and charged with the murder.

At his subsequent trial, Heywood readily confessed to the killing of Ann Turner. He said she was a witch and had cast the evil eye on sheep and cattle, and that all the minor misfortunes of the immediate neighbourhood could be laid at her door. 'Her wus a proper old witch', claimed Heywood, 'and there be at least 16 in Long Compton' . He also claimed there were enough witches to draw a 'wagon load of hay up Long Compton Hill' and if you saw the steep rise of this hill, you would know this would be no mean feat. Except, of course, that if they were indeed witches, they could accomplish it by witchcraft!

Heywood maintained he had 'sticked' the witch, Ann Turner, and had drawn first blood in order to take away her power. Since Saxon times it has been understood that this was the only possible means of rendering a witch powerless, to practice 'stacung' and to draw first blood.

Heywood refused to express any remorse. He felt he had done the neighbourhood a service, and he asked in court that the body of Ann Turner should be weighed against the church bible; in his view this would prove beyond all shadow of doubt that the old woman was a witch. He claimed that if only she had been killed sooner, a great number of people now lying in Long Compton churchyard would still be alive.

Another legend, first recorded by John of Tynemouth in 1362 concerns the visit to Long Compton of St Augustine in AD 604. It seems that the parish priest of Long Compton was having a bit of bother with the lord of the town' who simply refused to pay his tithes. The priest admonished and eventually excommunicated the man, but all to no avail. His tithes remained unpaid.

The parish priest therefore went trotting off to talk the matter over with St Augustine, who accompanied him back to his home at Long Compton. St Augustine had a little chat with the lord of the town, but again he refused to pay his tithes so the saint excommunicated him again. St Augustine then proceeded to take mass in the church, and he said 'I command that no excommunicate person be present at this mass'. Whereupon a grave near to the church wall opened and a dead man arose from it, standing quietly outside the church wall as the service proceeded.

Afterwards, the saint came towards the man and asked him what he did in that place. The man said he had lived there in the time of the Britons and refusing to pay his tithes, was excommunicated by the priest of the time. When he died, he was therefore thrust into hell. He then pointed out to St Augustine the grave of the priest who had excommunicated him all those many years before. Nothing loath, the saint raised the priest from the dead and proceeded to question him. After hearing the full story from both, the saint took pity upon the excommunicate and granted him absolution. Thus his heavenly future assured, the figure crumpled into dust at the saint's feet and was no more. St Augustine then turned to the priest and asked him if he would like to return to earth to continue with his preaching and to do God's work. The man explained he had been in his grave for 150 years and he had no wish to enter once more into this troubled world. So the saint dismissed him back to eternity.

Having performed all this, the saint then turned to the troublesome lord of the town and said 'Wilt thou not pay thy due tithes, my son'. Whereupon the troublesome fellow fell upon his knees, craved pardon for all his many sins, paid his tithes (probably back-dated!) and sinned no more!

Long Itchington

➤ It was in this place, called by the Anglo-Saxons 'the farm by the river Itchen, that St Wulfstan was born early in the 11th century. He was of fairly humble parentage, and yet received an education better than most of his class and station. He was a friend of Lady Godiva, the benefactress who rode naked through the streets of Coventry in an effort to persuade her husband Leofric of the innate goodness of its citizens so that he might remove some of the swingeing taxes he had seen fit to impose upon them. Wulfstan was also a good friend to King Harold.

He was consecrated Bishop of Worcester in 1062, and helped to found Worcester Cathedral. When the Normans came, Wulfstan gave his allegiance to William the Conqueror. He worked assiduously, building, preaching, providing schools, and did perhaps more than any other man of his time to bring together Norman and Saxon in peace.

He opposed Lanfranc, the Norman Archbishop of Canterbury, who publicly declared Wulfstan did not have the background and education for his high office. But Wulfstan fought hard to hold what he felt to be his by right, and when Lanfranc asked Wulfstan to surrender his bishop's staff, he drove it with great force into the tomb of Edward the Confessor in Westminster Abbey. All efforts to remove it failed, until Lanfranc literally begged Wulfstan to take it back and resume office.

The few villagers at Long Itchington in those days probably heard very little of the labours of their most famous son, but it would be a very different case in 1572, by which time the village had grown to encompass several good houses, one of which, Tudor House, the home of the Lady Anne Holbourne, was busy making ready to receive a very special guest on 12th August. Elizabeth I the beloved Good Queen Bess, was to spend a night with the Lady Anne. She must have greatly enjoyed her brief visit, for three years later the village went into the same excited frenzy when in July 1575 she was expected back again, this time for a slightly longer visit.

The peasants and labourers must have stood around open

mouthed at the great activity on the village green, for Robert Dudley, Earl of Leicester, was the host this time. And the great earl seldom did anything by halves! A vast tent was put up on the green in the middle of the little 'town' and all kinds of entertainment was organised to please Her Majesty. Robert Dudley was ever one for pleasing the ladies, and none so much as Good Queen Bess.

A contemporary description exists of this tent, 'which for number and shift of large and goodlye rooms might be comparable with a beautiful pallais. . .'. And into all this went jesters, jugglers, performers, cooks, scullions, confections and comestibles, and last of all the Queen herself. The jollification lasted several days, and then the royal retinue continued on its way to the castle of Kenilworth, where Robert Dudley had organised another whole week of junketings. Long Itchington was left to gather up the scraps, and to watch the great tent as big as a 'pallais' removed from their green. Doubtless they all enjoyed themselves.

The Tudor House is still in Long Itchington. It must have been fairly newly built in the great Queen's time and it has obviously been extensively altered. It still faces the village green upon which roads have now encroached, and many of the elm trees which once fringed the village pond have alas perished, as with many of our 'Warwickshire weeds'.

Something which met with considerably less approbation in Long Itchington was a club which started towards the end of the 19th century. The 'Deadnaps Club' caused a great deal of mischief, for they would march through the village bearing upon their banner the legend 'Able to work but not willing'. They were more or less dedicated topers, and one of their fanciful initiation ceremonies was a dunking in the Itchen.

Their pranks and hoaxes were more of a nuisance than based upon any malice, but one weekend they went a bit too far. Late one Saturday night they came upon an old donkey peaceably grazing in a field. The donkey was always there, too old to be of much further use, but held in affection by the old dame, its owner. With the aid of ropes, and with what must be acknowledged as a great deal of cunning, the donkey was caught and hoisted up on the church roof. The topers themselves were far too full of good cheer to recognise any inherent dangers. The pathetic animal, braying pitifully, was left stranded.

Early the following morning, villagers emerging from their homes asked each other 'What was all the noise in the night, it sounded like the old dame's donkey?' But no one knew the answer. No one thought where to look. That is until they all set off f for morning service in church, when to their utter amazement they were confronted with the terrified and braying donkey slithering about on the roof of their church. It took several days to get the creature safely down, but happily it is on record that it came to no real harm, and was speedily returned to the good dame.

The Deadnaps Club didn't last very long after this. I suppose it really was one of the forerunners of similar groups of youths in our midst today. But Long Itchington has had to live down the story of the donkey on the church roof!

Lower Quinton

The Quintons, Upper and Lower, on the boundary of Warwickshire and Gloucestershire, duster on the slopes of Meon Hill, immortalised by the poet Michael Drayton in his *Polyolbion* (1613). These villages, or more accurately a village and a hamlet, used to be in Worcestershire, until one of the inevitable local government boundary changes earlier this century, when the residents woke up one morning and discovered they lived in Warwickshire. This upset them thoroughly, and they roundly declared they didn't want to live in Warwickshire because the weather was much colder than in their native Worcestershire!

Meon Hill is beautiful, with wooded copses, sheep grazing, harebells and grasses blowing in the soft spring breeze. But it also has its darker side for it has always been associated with witchcraft, and it has been whispered that Shakespeare took the three witches' scene in *Macbeth* from his visits to Lower Quinton and Meon Hill.

In any case, the old legend tells us that Meon Hill was created by the Devil! The land used to be flat, but one day Old Nick stood upon nearby Ilmington Hill and saw workmen building a great abbey church some miles away at Evesham. He didn't like this idea at all and in a rage he gave a great kick and sent a huge pile of earth upwards intending that it should fall upon the abbey and bury it forever. But good St Egwin was watching and acted promptly, arresting the flight of the earth so that it all fell down and became Meon Hill.

The top of the hill was the site of an ancient camp, with pit dwellings dating from the Iron Age, but bits and pieces from the earlier Neolithic age have also been discovered on the site. The Roman historian Tacitus knew Meon Hill, and described it as one of a line of camps stretching right across the country.

There was a legend of buried treasure on Meon Hill. It is the kind of place where such legends proliferate, and the story goes that a farm labourer of the last century discovered a pot of gold upon Meon Hill. He kept quiet about it, went away, bought his own farm and became very prosperous. In the early 1800s some excavations carried out on the site of the old camp did reveal treasure, but of a more unusual kind. Celtic currency in the form of pieces of iron, shaped like blades. Meon Hill is now under cultivation and has been so for many years. This has more or less obliterated the traces of the ancient camp.

It has its resident ghost, of course. The story goes that a local man was so obsessed with hunting that he kept his own pack of hounds, and enjoyed the chase almost every day. Despite protests from the Church he refused to refrain from his hunting exploits even on the Sabbath. So upon one Sabbath, vengeance was wreaked upon him. In full cry the pack careered across Meon Hill, with their master, when suddenly the earth opened wide and a great yawning pit appeared. Master and hounds all disappeared into it, and the earth closed above their heads. Still on Sundays, when the moon is full and darkness gathers around the venerable crown of Meon Hill, it is said that the huntsman and his pack ride in the eternal chase to which they were doomed.

The name Quinton in Saxon means 'Manor of Women' and

this derives from the fact that there was a Benedictine nunnery at Upper Quinton. Few traces remain except for ancient stones incorporated into the walls of old houses, and part of an old stone causeway across a field leading from the old site to the south door of the church of St Swithin in Lower Quinton.

Old records tell us that Egbert, King of Wessex, was so overjoyed at his son's recovery from a near fatal illness that he set up a nunnery at Polesworth in the north of Warwickshire. His daughter Edith entered the nunnery, and at the same time they received the gift of the lands at Quinton. She decided that the church at Lower Quinton should be dedicated to St Swithin because Swithin (or Swithun) had been tutor to Edith's brother, Ethelwulf.

The nunnery at Upper Quinton became quite a rich one and lasted for many years. Its most notable anchorite was Joan, Lady Clopton. Her husband, Sir William Clopton fought at the battle of Agincourt in 1415, and died four years later in 1419. He has a stone effigy in the south arcade of the church of St Swithin. When he died, his widow Joan was apparently bothered by unwelcome suitors. After all she was still young and fairly rich. So in order to get rid of them all, she took vows of perpetual widowhood before a bishop and entered the nunnery at Upper Quinton. She devoted her life to good works, paid for much of the church and for the spire on top of the tower, once 130 ft high but now only 127 ft, which has become a landmark for miles in all directions.

She died in 1430 and is buried in the chapel of St Anne at Quinton, beneath a table tomb on top of which is one of the finest brasses in the county, with a Latin inscription exhorting 'Christ, grandson of Anne, have mercy on Joan Clopton'. She was, we are told, generous to hapless children and unstinting to strangers.

Plague came to Quinton in 1556 and in May 26 villagers succumbed to this dread disease. In total 58 out of 250 inhabitants died in that year, and within living memory the old plague pits were discovered within the churchyard, as new graves were dug.

Loxley

No one could claim that Loxley is a pretty village. All that rural 'roses round the door' has no place here. Yet it is peaceful and quiet, and set amid some quite breathtaking views across the Avon valley to the far distant Malvern Hills.

The village straggles down the hill, and at the bottom is Loxley church, built by the Normans. It fortunately escaped the restoration of the Victorian era and instead was restored a century before, so that it now presents an almost untouched Georgian interior, complete with box pews and a strange pulpit arrangement so that the vicar emerging from the vestry pops up' into the pulpit like a Jack-in-the-Box. On the ancient tower is a notable sundial which tells us 'I die today and live tomorrow'.

But it is the churchyard at Loxley that attracts so many visitors, for every spring it is a veritable carpet of snowdrops, called in Warwickshire 'Fair Maids of February', aconites, primroses and anemones.

This is the last church in Warwickshire to keep up the old wedding custom of 'barring the way', which used to be much more widespread but has now almost entirely died out. When a newly married couple emerge from Loxley's St Nicholas's church, they are likely to find the church gates securely fastened with ropes or garlands of wild flowers, or tendrils of ivy. It is the groom's job to unfasten them for his bride, symbolising that he will henceforth make her path clear. Sometimes the groom can pay a small forfeit by scattering a few coins for charity. It is a pretty custom, taking place in one of the prettiest churchyards in the whole of the county.

Most of the village clusters around the old Fox Inn, dating in part from the 17th century, and like all good inns, the Fox is not without its ghost. Old Percy used to keep the village post office and every evening at precisely a quarter to nine o'clock, he came into the inn, and invariably paid for his drinks from a five shilling bag of coppers which he up-ended on the counter. Long after old Percy died, the door by which he was wont to enter the inn every evening invariably swung open at a quarter to nine.

Regulars got well used to this phenomenon, and merely remarked to each other 'Percy's on time as usual'.

However, since the days of Old Percy the inn has undergone some alterations, and the door through which Percy entered, both before and after his death, no longer exists . Therefore, if he still comes in to spend a pleasant evening in the surroundings he used to know so well, he must needs slip in unnoticed.

This Loxley is said to have been the birthplace of the great outlaw who robbed the rich to give to the poor – Robin Hood, or Robin of Loxley. No one will ever know for certain, but it is not entirely impossible.

Loxley was given by the great King Offa of the Mercians to the monks of Worcester some three centuries before William brought his Norman invaders to our shores. But in the time of the Danish King Canute, they lost it. The whole realm groaned beneath the weight of terrible taxation, and Canute decreed that taxes must be paid on the due day. If they were not, then any man could pay the taxes on the land and it would then belong to him. The monks didn't pay their dues for Loxley on the appropriate day, and consequently it passed into other hands.

By the time the 12th century dawned, and Henry II was king, a man named Robert fils Odonis, or Robert FitzOdo owned Loxley. He seems to have been a pious and good man, for he made many grants to various religious houses. It is certain that he lived at Loxley, where he built himself a 'mannour' house which his grandson ultimately gave to the monks of Kenilworth.

Now was this Robert FitzOdo the celebrated Robin Hood? The place is right, the date is right, and with a little imagination Robert FitzOdo could be translated into 'Robin Hood'. Sadly there is no trace of the manor house which he built for himself, and where he lived.

Moreton Morrell

➤ Moreton Morrell lies just off the Fosse Way, and overlooks the valley of the Avon. Much of the village is old, with Still some ancient thatch, but is not now so quiet as it must once have been when the manor house was the retreat of the sad and ill-fated Amy Robsart.

Poor Amy, wife of Robert Dudley, Earl of Leicester, the favourite of the powerful Queen Elizabeth, was kept severely in the background by her husband, and never seems to have taken her rightful place at his side. They were married in 1550, but by the time Dudley had been taken up by Elizabeth, Amy was becoming perhaps something of a hindrance to his ambition. Small wonder then that she dung to a lifelong friendship with Mary, daughter of Sir William Flammock, and wife of John Colebourne of Moreton Morrell. She often stayed with Mary in this small village while her husband was busily engaged on the Queen's business, and it is believed that her last visit was in 1558, two years before her sudden and lonely death at Cumnor Place in 1560. It was commonly thought that her death was murder, engineered by her ambitious husband and his cohorts, but a subsequent enquiry failed to resolve the issue.

The relatively humble family of Randolph lived in Moreton Morrell too, and William Randolph was born here in 1650. At the age of 22, William decided to emigrate to Virginia, USA, to strike out and make a new life for himself. He succeeded, married, founded a family and his grand-daughter Jane married Peter Jefferson. Their son, Thomas Jefferson was born in 1743 at Shadwell, Albemarle County Virginia. After an illustrious career he became President of the United States from 1801 to 1809. He it was who helped to draft the Declaration of Independence which was signed on 4th July 1776.

This is not the only American connection within this small village though. It is virtually dominated by Moreton Hall, a superb mansion situated on a gentle hill and once surrounded by trees and parkland. At first glance, the casual passer-by might be forgiven for thinking the Hall had been sitting here for centuries, but this is not the case. Indeed, it has yet to make its first century!

It was in 1905 that an American millionaire, Mr Charles Tuller Garland bought this land and proceeded to build himself a very grand house and an estate to go with it. The architect of the Hall was Mr Romaine Walker, who designed this Georgian-style pile, and built it of bathstone. There were many lavish appointments, superb panelling and quite fantastic marble bathrooms, the remains of which still exist. The grounds were wonderfully laid out, and every sporting requirement of Mr Garland, his family and friends was more than adequately catered for. There were sunken gardens, arboretums, vineries and pleasure gardens, probably causing some astonishment among the villagers at the time.

Mr Garland also built for himself a real tennis club, just opposite the end of his drive. Purists will tell us there is no such thing as real tennis, only tennis and lawn tennis. This club building is Edwardian complete with gargoyles and parapets. There are mammoth baths and showers, faded photographs, and a court described as 'fast and true'. It is now run as a successful club, with many dedicated members and friends.

In March 1920 the grand estate of Moreton Hall was sold to Colonel Ogilby, in whose possession it remained until he put it on the market in 1938. But with the onset of the war a year later it was used for billetting soldiers. Americans, British and Czechs were housed in the Hall and on the estate. Indeed, the newspapers of the time called it the birthplace of the Free Czech Army.

Warwickshire County Council bought the estate in 1948 and established their successful Institute of Agriculture. Much work had to be done, and the first 60 students were welcomed for a one year course in November 1949. Since that time it has gone from strength to strength, offering full time courses in various aspects of agriculture, horse management and related subjects to students from all over the world. But the facade of Mr Garland's Hall remains unchanged and still looks out upon a pleasurable view, except that instead of servants and sportsmen scurrying to and fro, there are now students and lecturers; instead of pleasure gardens and vineries, there are now farm buildings and stables.

Newbold Pacey

Here in the 14th century came that dread marauder, the Black Death, and decimated the village. It carried off so many that the village has never properly recovered and is now little more than a hamlet.

A particularly delightful hamlet, though. And the lane that leads the way to the church of St George the Martyr takes you almost out of this world and deposits you in the midst of an idyllic green, with Thelsford brook separating Newbold from its adjoining parish of Ashorne.

On your left is a Queen Anne rectory, almost hidden behind tall brick walls, and in front is the church, rebuilt in 1881 by J. L. Pearson, the architect of Truro Cathedral. He did, however, re-use two Norman doorways, and architectural experts describe the church as a 'rustic pile' with an unusual saddle-backed roof tower.

The parish registers contain the note that in 1554, just when Mary Tudor had ascended the throne of England, and was beginning her persecution of those she considered heretics, 'John Puncheon became vicar. Mr Hilton leaving the place because he was a Protestant and married'. Almost a century later, in 1642 'a souldier wounded in that great battell between ye King and the parliament Oct 23rd was buried ye Oct 29th'. This refers to the Battle of Edgehill, of course. The 'souldier' must have made it as far as Newbold Pacey, where he lingered for six days.

The Great Plague was still raging in 1668, and a gentleman called Edward Carew fled from the city to take refuge with his family at Newbold Pacey. Alas, he brought the plague with him, and here he remained. He gazes down from the south wall of the church, with his tiny infant daughter in front of him. Edward Carew 'put off his vail of mortality' in the 46th year of his age; his tiny daughter Felicia lived but 13 days. They were buried together on 16th November 1668.

High upon the wall in the chancel is a memorial tablet to Thomas Castle Southey, vicar here from 1868 until 1899. He was the son of Captain Thomas Southey, and nephew of the poet Robert Southey. He too may have tried his hand at verse, but whether or not he wrote his own epitaph I have not discovered. It says simply:

> Lay me my friends beside the yews I planted
> My slumbering friends around
> But when at morning tide new life is granted
> Within this hallowed ground
> To shepherd and sheep, I trust I may arise
> From tranquil sleep midst those I prize.

Outside, quite close, are five ancient clipped yews. He may well have planted them during his vicarate, when his church was rebuilt. Or perhaps he was using a snippet of poetic licence. It doesn't really matter. He remained here and obviously cared for his flock for 33 years, and didn't want to leave.

Newbold Revel

It is always romantic to hear tales of daring-do; of gallant rescues and heroic escapades. English history is peopled with the perpetrators of such deeds and most of us like it that way, even if we do take some of it with a large pinch of salt.

However, we did have a real life swashbuckler right here in Warwickshire; a man whose escapades made him a legend in his own lifetime, and who eventually turned out to be the author of one of the most famous works in the English language.

Sir Thomas Malory lived at Newbold Revel a lovely old mansion house close to the village of Monks Kirby in the north of the county. The old house is now gone, replaced with a more fashionable structure in 1716 which was later refurbished and turned into a college. The old house came into the possession of the Malory family through a judicious marriage, and Sir Thomas inherited in 1433.

He served courageously as a soldier with Richard Beauchamp, Earl of Warwick, and spent many years with him in France, during which time he gathered many romantic stories and legends of Knights Errant and their chivalrous deeds. He took part in tourneys and he learned of the Arthurian legends, the quest for the Holy Grail, and the problems of Sir Lancelot. He loved these stories, and he kept them all within his heart and head.

Eventually he returned to this country and to Newbold Revel. But at this time the country was at its most lawless. King Henry VI was unable to control his nobles, who had become used to fighting in the French campaigns, and the houses of York and Lancaster were at each other's throats. In 1454 the King succumbed to the madness that threatened him, and Richard Duke of York was appointed Regent. The following years were bloody and turbulent.

Among all of it rode Sir Thomas Malory of Newbold Revel. He became a law breaker himself and it was not long before he was well on his way to a career of violence. He acted without scruple, even within his own parish, despite the fact he was three times Member of Parliament for Warwickshire, and his 'undercover' escapades continued. He was not choosy; he had a go at anything, including ambush, murder, cattle stealing, armed robbery, rape and extortion.

One night with a band of cronies he forced his way into Coombe Abbey, near Coventry, and stole as much money and as many church ornaments as he could carry off with him. He obviously then decided this plunder was not quite enough, for he returned the following day, frightened the gentle and quiet monks out of their wits, and made off with everything else.

In Monks Kirby itself, the Carthusian brothers were terrorised and robbed, and there seemed little anyone could do about it. There was no law to enforce, and people seemed to think it better to keep their mouths shut and their heads down, while awaiting better times.

On 21st July 1451, following bitter complaints from the Prior of Epworth, who was getting a bit fed up with not getting his proper share of tithes from Monks Kirby because they had all been stolen, Sir Thomas Malory was arrested. Armed men rode up to his home at Newbold Revel and took him prisoner.

They took no chance with this one. He had been around too long, and it was in chains he was carted off to Coleshill Hall, home of the de Monforts, where he was flung into a dungeon. He must have realised he didn't have much chance if he came to trial; his crimes had been too numerous. He remained in prison only two days. He managed to get free of his gaolers, and under cover of darkness leapt into the deep moat surrounding the Hall and swam for his very life.

As soon as he could, he resumed his lawless life, even more audaciously than before. But eventually he went too far, and was once again taken prisoner, charged with sedition against the King and in 1468 found himself languishing in Newgate from which there really was no escape.

Here in this dreadful noisome prison, dank, evil smelling and comfortless, Sir Thomas thought again of the great days of chivalry; of the tales he had so often heard. He wrote it all down. Perhaps he felt in some way it was a kind of atonement, or even an explanation, for his misdeeds.

Here in Newgate, he wrote *Morte d'Arthur*; a prose translation from the French, with adaptations from other sources. Certainly, the companions who rode with Sir Thomas in the Wars of the Roses are all here, transformed into legend. This was, perhaps, the world Malory wanted, and not the lawless one he had been forced to inhabit.

He died in Newgate, and was buried close by in the chapel of St Francis at Greyfriars. The plain stone above him reads 'Sir Thomas Mallore, valiant Knight, died 14th March 1470, of the parish of Monkenkyrby in the County of Warwick'.

Sixteen years passed, and in 1486 Caxton printed Malory's work. In his notes he remarks it was a book 'reduced into English by Sir Thomas Malory, Knight, in the 9th year of the reign of Edward IV'. But at that time there were three Sir Thomas Malorys in various places, and it was open to doubt whether or not it was the swashbuckler of Newbold Revel who produced this work. The matter was finally settled in 1934 when a manuscript was discovered in the library of Winchester College, said to be a copy of the original made by Caxton before going to press, and including bits he eventually had to omit. This, according to experts proved beyond a shadow of doubt that *Morte d' Arthur,* called by Sir Walter Scott 'the best prose romance the English language can boast of', was indeed the work of Warwickshire's own Sir Thomas Malory, soldier, idealist, outlaw, swashbuckler, and owner of Newbold Revel.

Newnham Paddox

➤ Newnham Paddox was once the home of the Earls of Denbigh, who over centuries have faithfully served successive monarchs. But alas, the great house no longer exists. It was demolished in 1952 when a series of tragic family bereavements brought in their wake such crippling death duties that the house could no longer be maintained.

The wrought iron gates believed to have been made by the famous Welsh Davies brothers, elaborate with birds and dragons, may still be seen about a mile outside the village of Monks Kirby in the north of the county, but the house and the church, rebuilt in the substantial and handsome style of the 19th century, have gone forever.

The Fieldings were originally associated with Lutterworth in Leicestershire, and came into the possession of Newnham by a judicious marriage with the heiress of Robert of Newnham in 1433. The Fieldings believe they were descended from the Hapsburgs of Germany, with Sir Geoffrey reputed to be the dispossessed son of an Earl of Hapsburg, Lord of Laufenburg and Rheinfeldon, for reason of a family feud, the causes of which are lost in the mists of time.

Sir Geoffrey fought for Henry III and was rewarded. Upon his marriage to Maud Colville, an heiress, he took the name Fielding. Whether it was derived from 'Rheinfeldon' or taken because it was the name of his wife's step-mother, of whom she was very fond, has never been made clear. The Hapsburg claim has been questioned, but not until the latter half of the 19th century, when the authenticity of some of the 14th century family documents came under scrutiny. As one of the family put it at the time, they are quite content to be 'Perhapsburgs'.

The family was fortunate, or perhaps careful, in whom they chose to marry. Sir William Fielding's wife, Susan, was the sister of the notorious George Villiers, later Duke of Buckingham. Villiers, known throughout the court as 'Steenie', a pet name bestowed upon him by King James I, found such high favour with that monarch that honours and riches were literally heaped upon him. Small wonder then that he advanced his sister's husband. Sir William became first Baron, then Viscount Fielding of Newnham Paddox, and in 1622 was created Earl of Denbigh.

The onset of the Civil War split the family asunder, for Denbigh was a Royalist and fought for King Charles I at the Battle of Edgehill, whereas his son, Basil, took the opposite side and fought for Parliament. Father and son met head on on the battlefield. This caused Lady Denbigh, wife of one and mother of the other, desperate distress. The Earl was mortally wounded in a skirmish at Birmingham a year later in 1643, and died of his injuries three days later. Lady Denbigh's sorrow, not only upon the death of her husband, but because of the estrangement and different loyalties between father and son, are revealed in letters she wrote at this time.

She too had her share of misfortune, for she was Lady of Honour to Queen Henrietta Maria and became her close friend and confidante, later going into exile in France. Here she met the poet Crashaw, who dedicated much of his pious work to her. She became a Catholic just before she died in 1652.

Basil, the wayward son, now the second Earl was a much travelled and highly intellectual man. He had served Charles I as a diplomat, and assisted that sad monarch in the collection of treasures of art. With the Restoration, he was reconciled to Charles II and thus managed to retain all his estates and titles. Although he married four times, he left no issue when he died in 1674.

Of this family came Henry Fielding, author of Tom Jones. The family jokingly said of him that he was the first one who could spell! The Denbighs continued at Court, and lived the fairly uneventful lives of their kind and times. In 1840, the seventh Earl took a house at Bushey Park near London, and Newnham was let to produce more money. Its tenant was Joseph Buonapart, brother of Napoleon, and ex-King of Spain.

The ninth Earl lost two of his three sons in the First World War, and his surviving son died in 1937, pre-deceasing his father by two years. When the Earl died Newnham ceased to be a family home, and although the family still survives in the area, the grand house at Newnham Paddox is no more.

Offchurch

When nearby Leamington Spa was but a simple settlement, Offchurch was important, for its location is close to the Fosse Way and not far from the Welsh Road, the long distance bridleway from Anglesey used by cattle drovers in the pre-motor transport, pre-railway ages. These wary men drove their beasts along roundabout ways to avoid having to pay excessive tolls on turnpike routes, and the Welsh Road took them through Offchurch on their way to Southam, where the route, although now a well used highway, is still called 'Welsh Road'.

Offchurch is a tucked away place, the lanes running through the village are narrow and curving, lined with mellow brick houses and verdant gardens, leading to its church on a hill.

This is Offa's Kingdom, for here lived the great Saxon warrior king (AD 757-796) who made his realm of Mercia the most powerful in the land. Charlemagne called him the 'greatest of all western kings'. He built himself a palace, or perhaps as some say it was more like a hunting lodge, where the river Leam sweeps in a wide curve. The site is now occupied by a lovely old house with parkland, known as Offchurch Bury. Within its grounds were discovered hollow stone capitals thought at one time to be a part of Offa's ancient palace. However, experts decided they were not that ancient, but Byzantine in character, much resembling the arcades of the church of St Sophia at Constantinople. They are said to be 'not later than 11th century'.

Offa founded the church in memory of his son, Fremund. Prince Fremund is described by the chronicler Camden, as 'a man of great renowne and singular piety to Godward, unto whom nothing else procured envie and evill will, but because in an unhappy time hee had by happy conduct quelled the audacious courage of his enemies'. Poor Fremund was foully murdered on a barren heath between Long Itchington and Harbury, almost within sight of his father's house. It is likely there was a skirmish at this spot between Fremund's men and his enemies, for many Saxon relics were found buried here.

The murdered body of Offa's beloved son was carried to Offchurch, and legend has it that he was buried here. Certainly there was an ancient burial ground on the site of the present church, for in 1866-7 many skeletons were uncovered, and the weapons and jewellery found to have been buried with them set the date at around AD 650, a century before Offa became king.

Legend also has it that the great Offa himself was buried at Offchurch, outside the church he built in Fremund's memory. The present church, dedicated to St Gregory, is basically Early English and partly Norman, but undoubtedly stands upon the site of a much earlier building.

When restoration work was undertaken in the middle of the 19th century, a coffin lid believed to be that of King Offa was found built into the chancel wall. It is of such design that it must have been made for someone of importance, and could have been used for the body of either Offa or his son, Fremund. Two sand stones, their carvings much eroded, were also found built into the north wall of the nave, and it is thought these must have been part of another coffin of some importance. Local tradition insists that these two discoveries lend weight to the idea that both Offa and Fremund were buried at Offchurch, where they lived. But this belief has never been officially confirmed. On the other hand, neither has it been officially discounted!

Offchurch did not entirely escape in the Civil War, for the 14th century church tower is marked by stray musket balls from a minor skirmish in August 1642. It seems King Charles I rode through this village on his way to Oxford, guided by three Offchurch men, who were each thanked by His Majesty and paid a farthing each for their trouble.

Offchurch Bury, where Offa's palace or lodge once stood, was given to the monks of Coventry after the Conquest, and upon the Dissolution of the Monasteries passed to Sir Edmund Knightley, one of the King's commissioners appointed to deal with the Dissolution. The older parts of the house date from this period, but it was largely rebuilt in the 19th century and is now mostly of the fashionable 1829 Gothick.

Offchurch has many ghosts; how could it be otherwise with the murder and mayhem of the Saxon factions. But it also has a more recent apparition. In the 17th century a man was stabbed to death outside the church of St Gregory. Why he was done to death we do not know, but the man who stabbed him ran into the church for sanctuary, and was seen in the tower. He managed to escape under cover of darkness and was never seen again. But the ghost of the murdered man has been seen, wandering around the tower seeking his own murderer, and his search has sometimes been accompanied by the mournful muffled tolling of the church bell.

Over Whitacre

━━ Strange it is to relate how a man's life should hang upon something as trivial as the shape of a patch upon the knee of his breeches. Yet this is exactly what happened to Isaac Brindley in 1810 in the Warwickshire village of Over Whitacre.

Over Whitacre now is a victim of industry and affords nothing more than a view of Ham's Hall cooling towers, although it does still have a Baroque steeple to its church, and a superb black-and-white timbered house, Botts Green House, built in 1593 and incredibly beautiful.

The outlook was very different when Isaac Brindley and Nancy Smith worked for the Weston family in the big house at Over Whitacre. On the morning of 11 th October 1809, William

Beresford, gardener to the Weston household, turned up for his day's work as usual and Mrs Weston came out of the house to ask him if he had seen anything of Nancy Smith. Beresford replied that he had not, and Mrs Weston was obviously a bit upset. She told him that on the previous evening, the 10th October, she had sent Nancy over to a neighbour, a Mr Lax, with a jug of balm (fermenting yeast liquor). The girl set off upon her errand and had not been seen since. Mrs Weston was worried about her, and instructed Beresford to go and see if he could see any sign of the girl before he started his work. Accordingly, off set Beresford in the direction Nancy must have taken the evening before.

He had not gone far when he came to a pit by the roadside, and upon a piece of headland, left at the end of the furrows after ploughing, he saw a woman's shoe standing upright. The ground near by was much trampled, and Beresford noticed that there was a lot of wheat and chaff scattered around.

Beresford stooped to pick up the shoe and he noticed near to it the clear imprint of the knee of a man's breeches upon the ground, and close by the heel of a man's shoe. The breeches must have been made of cord, and a patch had been put on them of a different pattern of cord. Beresford glanced at the pit, and to his horror saw two female arms. He looked closer and discovered the missing Nancy Smith, lying upon her back in the pit, with her head towards the field.

Beresford, much shaken, ran back to tell Mrs Weston and to get help to recover the poor girl from the pit. It seems Nancy Smith never got as far as the Lax household, for the jug and the balm were found spilled upon the ground.

Nancy Smith had been strangled, and there were livid bruises upon her neck. Her arms were badly scratched, and Mr Thomas Barker, surgeon, said she must have been completely pulled through the hedge before being cast into the pit. The body continued to bleed from the ear and the mouth three days after being taken up, but the surgeon declared this to be quite usual in cases of strangulation.

It appears that when Nancy Smith had been about to leave the Weston household, she had asked her fellow servant, Isaac

Brindley, if he would carry her box up to William Beresford's house. Beresford had offered to keep it for her until she got settled in a new post. Brindley agreed, and knocked on Beresford's door at about eight o'clock on the night of the 10th October, with the box on his shoulder. Beresford told him where to put it, and noticing that Brindley was in a considerable sweat, offered him a drink. But Brindley refused saying he was tired and was off home to bed. Questioned about his movements on the night of the 10th October, Brindley stupidly told lies, declaring himself to have been with a friend. But this didn't check out, because the 'friend' was 30 miles off and in another job at that particular time.

Another servant said she had helped Brindley to lift Nancy's box, but this was at six o'clock in the evening. Beresford's house was no more than ten minutes off, and he didn't arrive there until around eight o'clock. It was quite obvious that Nancy, off to the Lax household with the balm, and Brindley on his way to Beresford's house, must have met, since both houses lay in the same direction, and they could scarcely have missed each other.

Another servant, William Teag, rather surprised the court when he told how he had seen Brindley and Nancy Smith in a small stable two weeks prior to the murder. Nancy was crying, and Brindley had his arms around her. It is clear there was a relationship between the two, a relationship that had been kept completely secret from their fellow servants.

A tailor was called to examine the patch on the knee of Brindley's working breeches, and it was found to exactly match the impression left on the ground near the pit. So did the mark of the shoe match those Brindley wore for work. The wheat and chaff was explained by the fact that Brindley had been employed threshing the whole of the day of the 10th October.

The court decided that despite Brindley's assertion that he 'knew nothing of the matter' he was guilty. They concluded he met Nancy near to the pit, and attempted to 'take liberties' (their own words) which were unwelcome to the girl. When she resisted, Brindley became angered, caught her around the throat and strangled her.

Brindley was sentenced to be hanged, and suffered the extreme penalty at Warwick on 11th April 1810. The pit where poor Nancy met her end was known as 'Nancy's hole' for some time afterwards, but it no longer exists.

Oxhill

Oxhill lies tucked snugly beneath the lee of the Edgehill escarpment, in the fertile and beautiful Vale of the Red Horse, where Warwickshire and Oxfordshire come together. The vale is so called because for centuries a giant horse figure 100 yards long and 70 yards high, cut out in the red soil of the hillside, was visible for miles. The horse, dating from Saxon times and a part of the ritual worship to the Great Horse God Tui, no longer gallops towards Sun Rising Hill. Sometime around the year 1800, the landlord of the local inn had the figure ploughed up to save himself the bother of scouring it annually. Needless to say, the landlord's selfish action was regarded with great disfavour and consequently his trade fell off alarmingly.

Oxhill is a small village, and slightly remote in the sense that it is not on the way to anywhere. The church of St Lawrence stands at the head of the village street, and is fortunate in that it has not suffered too badly at the hands of the restorer. On the south-east side of the churchyard is a gravestone that has aroused much speculation among historians, for it is believed to be the only slave's grave in the Midlands. The headstone above it was restored in 1969, and says:

Here lyeth the body of Myrtilla, negro slave to Mr Thos
Beauchamp of Nevis. Bapt. Oct ye 20th.
Buried Jan ye 6th 1705.

Mr Thomas Beauchamp of Nevis is thought to have been a sugar planter, but why he came to Oxhill is not known. At that time, the rector Nicholas Meese and his wife Jane had twin daughters, baptised in May 1677, with slightly unusual names, Margaretta and Perletta. Thomas Beauchamp married Perletta, and their infant daughter was baptised Margaretta after her aunt. Sadly, the little girl died when she was four years old, and is buried at Oxhill, with a memorial slab in front of the altar.

Four children were born to Thomas Beauchamp and his wife while they were in Oxhill, but after 1714 the names don't appear in any of the registers. Nicholas Meese died in 1715, after being rector of Oxhill and nearby Idlicote for 46 years, and his son, Walwyn, succeeded him. Perhaps it was at this time the Beauchamps decided to make a move.

Nicholas Meese buried poor Myrtilla, and recorded it thus in the burial register: 'Buried today a young negro girl belonging to Mrs Beauchamp'. He also records the baptism of one Will Archus 'an adult male black' in the year 1700, and in the registers for the parish of Idlicote, he records that he baptised 'a young negro girl (Margaret Lucy) belonging to ye Lady Underhulle'.

Grave of Myrtilla the slave, Oxhill

Myrtilla must have been regarded with affection by the Beauchamps, for they not only saw she was baptised, but decently buried with a good headstone to mark her last resting place. How a young girl from the sunny Leeward Islands must have viewed this tiny Warwickshire village in the 18th century cannot be imagined, and we do not know how old she was, nor how she died. Perhaps she was desperately homesick.

Electricity was installed in the church in 1967 and this event brought to light another curiosity, a 'maiden's wreath' thought to date from the 16th century, or perhaps earlier.

The ancient custom to which this refers was that when a maiden of the parish died, her friends wove a wreath from reeds, rushes or grasses, whatever was available, and interlaced with wild flowers. This was then suspended from the roof of the church, as near as possible to the place where the maiden sat for divine service. It was considered both unlucky and disrespectful to remove the wreath once it was hung, so that it was left in place until it rotted away. The fallen pieces were from time to time gathered up and strewn upon the maiden's grave.

The Oxhill wreath was certainly still hanging suspended when it was decided, presumably by the churchwardens of the time, to panel the inside of the roof. Workmen, fearful of ill luck, would not have removed the wreath, and so panelled it in. The subsequent exclusion of air obviously helped to preserve it. The strange thing about it is that this particular custom was thought never to have been observed in Warwickshire, and it has not been possible to find any other evidence of it anywhere in these parts. Therefore, how did it come to be used at Oxhill some 400 years ago? There is no mention in the parish records. Could it be that someone visited and brought the custom with them?

In 1967 when the wreath was discovered it was in a remarkable state of preservation, and after being examined by experts a glass case was made to completely enclose it and hopefully preserve it for even longer. The wreath hangs on the north wall inside the church.

The Pillertons

Pillerton Priors lies on the main Stratford to Banbury Road, and is so called because it once belonged to a Carthusian priory. Pillerton Hersey is down the hill on the road to Kineton. It was originally called Nether Pillerton, but in the 13th century the Hersey family took it over and gradually tacked their name upon it.

Pillerton Priors, straggling along a main road, can scarcely be called hidden, but tucked up a comer, just off a driveway leading to Sandpits Farm, is the old churchyard of St Mary Magdalene. It is approached by a pair of wooden gates, scarcely visible unless you know they are there, and the old churchyard, the grass scythed neatly, has many rows of ancient and leaning tombstones, with old coffin lids embedded in the day soil. You may imagine that you can trace the outlines of the church that once stood here, as I have often done, but in truth very little trace remains, for the church of St Mary Magdalene was burned down in 1666, the same time as the Great Fire of London.

How or why it caught fire is not known. Why it was never rebuilt also remains a mystery, but here and there in the hedges there are bits of stone which may have been a part of the old church. Pillerton Priors' families have been buried here for centuries, and still are, the latest date being 1984. There are the Stockleys, several generations at Sandpits Farm, the Gardeners and the Waltons, names that are still with us.

There is a bit of a mystery about what happened to the church plate at the time of the fire. It seems to have disappeared. A few bits of carved stone may be noticed by the discerning, incorporated into nearby houses. Why not? It would have been wasteful to allow it to lie useless upon a barren site. But the last that was heard of the church plate was when a couple of dear old ladies, in the 18th century, were known to have been quite innocently using the chalice as a sugar bowl.

Pillerton Hersey, or Lower Pillerton, has some fine old houses looking on to a tiny village green, and a lovely old church near to the manor house, once the home of Rev Henry Mills, who inherited from his father. He was a rather vigorous parson, employing quite a lot of curates, and was still working and thoroughly active in his 95th year, just as his father was before him. He took over Pillerton in 1841, 'improved' the church, built a village school, and was altogether the archetypal Victorian parson. His descendant, always known simply as Miss Mills, lived in the manor house until her death. She was a skilled wood carver and much of her work may still be seen in the church.

In the churchyard, quite close to the gates, stands a most curious gravestone, bearing a rather quaint legend:

> Here lies old William Allibone
> Our Venerable Wheelwright gone
> Oft as each Christian neighbour fell
> Studious he shaped each homely shell
> To order of the passing bell
> And each poor soul he gently gave
> On slackened cordage to the grave
> Foremost in many a funeral throng
> Himself resolved in mercy long
> Say shall the tombstone tell his praise
> And vaunt him marvel of his days
> Or shall it sorrowing confess
> Our best alas but worthlessness
> And trust the saviour to atone
> For sins unconquered, fault unknown
> For faith unfinished, work undone
> By poor old William Allibone.

Who composed this verse or how it was paid for, when Allibone was obviously a humble artisan, I know not. But after years of being overgrown and illegible, it has recently been recut and now presents to the world a face as shining as that of good old William.

Pillerton does have its ghost; quite a famous one. On the road towards Ettington, close to the parish boundary, is a small group of trees known as Mollsgrave Coppice. Moll, in this instance, was a poor gypsy girl who lived rough in the coppice. She may have been a little mad, for one moonlight night she drowned herself. Why, no one knows. The only thing they do know is that poor Moll still haunts Mollsgrave Coppice, screaming her head off on nights when the moon is full!

Preston-on-Stour

Near the windings of the river Stour, close to where it throws itself over a little weir, and behind the great house of Alscot Park, Preston-on-Stour may be found, but it will need to be sought for it considers itself very fortunate that it is not on the way to anywhere, and you have to come out of it the same way that you go in. It is mostly a Victorian estate village, tranquil, peaceful, unspoiled and with an enviable symmetry that has so far successfully evaded destruction.

It gathers around a wide village green, and straggles nonchalantly around a couple of looped lanes. Fine black and white timbered houses jostle gladly with the estate cottages, built of sturdy Victorian brick with hexagonal-paned windows and fish-scale tiled roofs in 1850. Each one had its pig sty and brewhouse behind, and its neat little garden with a wooden fence or a low brick wall at the front, and a yew tree by the garden gate.

The village got its name through ancient associations with the monastery of Deerhurst in Gloucestershire, and was originally called 'Priest's Towne'. Alscot Park is built upon the site of the old monastery, and of a deserted medieval village.

Both Alscot Park and the village have to thank a London

lawyer named James West for their pleasant face. James West was a 'Georgian grandee', Secretary to the Treasury, dedicated antiquary, man of letters; a cultivated intellectual who gathered about him friends with similar interests. He lived with his wife Sarah, at The Piazza, Covent Garden, where he filled his spare time collecting rare books and manuscripts. James West bought the house at Alscot Park in 1749 as a country retreat and Sarah wrote to friends that it was 'the comicallist little house you ever saw . . .'.

James West began by making dramatic alterations to the rather ordinary house at Alscot Park, transforming it from the 'comicallist' to the much more fashionable Gothick, with pointed windows and the odd battlement or two. He then turned his attention to the old church which stands amid fine trees on the hill rising from the village green in the centre of Preston-on-Stour. He paid £1,855 10s 0d to builder Edward Woodward of Chipping Campden to rebuild the chancel and the tower, and he set about discovering items with which to embellish its interior. He added finely carved woodwork, a wrought iron screen, and a collection of 16th century stained glass. Some of these have disappeared in the recurring fashion for improvement and restoration.

One curious item which seems to have no business there is a memorial tablet to Sir Nicholas Kempe (1621) and his two wives. As far as can be ascertained Nicholas Kempe had no connection whatever with Preston-on-Stour or Alscot Park. The memorial was originally in St Mary's church, Islington. James West seems to have taken a liking to it and simply brought it back to his own church.

When he died, his vast collection of books and manuscripts were sold. So many were there that it took the firm of auctioneers hired to do the job 24 solid days of selling. Some went to the Bodleian and some to the British Museums. Many went into private collections.

In 1848, his descendant James Roberts-West decided to turn Preston-on-Stour into a 'model village'. He pulled down some of the old cottages and built the present estate houses, and he built a school to serve the children of all who worked upon his estates. The school building remains, but is now used as a furniture workshop. Alscot Park is still the centre of the village, and is still owned by the descendants of the original James West.

Priors Marston

A Warwickshire border village on the slopes of Marston Hill and with superb views across neighbouring Northamptonshire, this is a quiet spot, close to the old Welsh Road used by drovers for driving their sheep from Wales to the London markets, thus managing to avoid many of the tolls exacted at the time.

Very little has been allowed to spoil Priors Marston, since it was designated as of importance in terms of conservation, and yet it is far from the sterile picture-book image. It is a working village, and a lively one, although many of the old cottages are now inhabited by commuters.

The flat and wide churchyard has many fine trees, but two great cedars dominate, their branches sweeping low to the ground. They are thought to be some two centuries old, although there are those who believe they are even older than this.

Inside the church on a window sill is the head of a 14th century cross, a particularly beautiful piece of stone sculpture, with rood figures of Our Lady, St John the Baptist, and Elizabeth. It is thought to have once stood upon a stone shaft in the churchyard, but no trace of this remains. Indeed, the head itself was lost for many years, until it was discovered buried deep in the garden of a village house and was given back to the church.

As you walk into the porch, you must perforce cross the memorial tablet to Richard West who died in 1691 and his wife Elizabeth who followed him three years later. It was a form of humility to be buried where all those who enter must walk over you, although why the Wests had reason to seek such humility is not known.

In 1863 the church was largely rebuilt, when Rev Prescott was the vicar, and a large stained glass window is a memorial to another of the same family. Admiral Sir Henry Prescott went into the Navy at the age of 13, fought many valorous sea battles, some against Napoleon, and remained in the service for 64 years, until he retired as Admiral at the age of 77. He lived on to end his days in Priors Marston at the ripe old age of 91.

The most famous craftsman of Priors Marston was Edward Gardiner, who had his workshop at Hillview, in the centre of this village. He was a part of the Cotswold Arts and Crafts movement at Sapperton in Gloucestershire, when Ernest Gimson and the Barnsleys started their workshops making simple farmhouse furniture in their own particular style. They were a part of the 'Anti-Scrape' movement and friends of William Morris and Philip Webb. At Pinbury Park, Sapperton, they opted out of what we now call the 'rat race' and lived the simple, rural life. Edward Gardiner was apprenticed to them, and learned how to make rush-seated chairs.

The movement lasted for quite a long time, but really ended with the death of Gimson. Edward Gardiner moved himself to a workshop at Priors Marston and continued to make Gimson chairs, just as he had always done, until his death in 1958. Fortunately, he took on an apprentice, Mr Neville Neal, who remained with him from 1939 until his death. Then Mr Neal carried on at Priors Marston for a couple of years, before moving to his own home village of Stockton, where he continues to make Gimson chairs, in exactly the same way, helped by his son, Lawrence. And so the Cotswold tradition may well have moved into Warwickshire, but it continues, and Gimson chairs are still sent all over the world.

Radway

Sheltered in the lee of the Edgehill escarpment, the main village street runs right through from the bottom of Sun Rising Hill to the opposite end, emerging at rising ground known as Knowle End.

The slopes of Edgehill form a superb, almost a painted backcloth to this pleasant village, with its wealth of old Hornton stone houses. The parish church of St Peter was removed from its original site and rebuilt on the opposite side of the village street in 1866, using all the old stones and windows from the original church, without any of them being in any way re-dressed. The gargoyles in the tower were discovered embedded some four or five feet in the old foundations of the original church.

Also removed, with the church, was the effigy to Kingsmill, killed in the Battle of Edgehill. Captain Henry Kingsmill fought for the King, and was 'slain by a cannon bullet'. His body was later recovered for burial and some years later, in 1670, when things had returned to normal after the Restoration, his mother Lady Bridget Kingsmill came from Sidmonton in the 'countie of Southampton', discovered her son's grave, and erected this monument to his memory. It was a handsome monument, but time has played with it a little and it is much worn and defaced. Legend has it that every year on the anniversary of the battle a small posy appears on the Kingsmill effigy, and no one knows who puts it there! The great white horse that he rode in the battle hasn't left either, but upon the anniversary can be seen, a misty shape, wandering across the battle site, searching for its dead master.

The monks of Stoneleigh had a cell at Radway in medieval times. It appears that the bracing air of these hills was considered beneficial, and those brethren in need of a bit of a pick-me-up were sent for a period of convalescence to Radway. Adjoining the monastic building was a tiny chapel and a graveyard. Until recently, bones were occasionally accidentally disinterred upon this spot.

Radway Grange is the 'big house' of the village, and is believed to have been built using some of the stones from the monastic buildings after the Dissolution. Here lived Sanderson Miller, the gentleman architect, who earned for himself the nickname 'Master of the Gothick'. His father made his fortune in Banbury, and acquired the Radway estate in 1712.

Sanderson Miller was an eccentric, and with wealth sufficient to pay for his foibles. Upon inheriting from his father, he began to transform the old grange, adding a new front in the Gothick style. He designed Hagley Hall for his friend George, First Lord

Lyttleton; he designed the great hall at Lacock Abbey in Wiltshire; he advised many friends on various embellishments to their old houses, and he built Warwickshire's own Shire Hall. He was a friend of the famous; a knowledgeable man of many ideas and a recognised agriculturalist. He gathered about him a circle of the most notable names of his day, and he dabbled in many things.

Upon the hillside he built a folly, the Radway Tower, set upon the exact spot where King Charles I's standard was raised upon that fateful day of 23rd October 1642. When the tower was completed in September 1750, Miller gave one of his famous parties. He was a very cordial and convivial host, and he welcomed a large assembly of local landowners, gentry and clergy to the extraordinary hexagonal room, with the roof emblazoned with the Royal arms and the arms of the Saxon heptarchy around the walls.

Henry Fielding, the novelist, was of the company and read aloud parts of his latest novel *Tom Jones*. The character of Squire Allworthy is supposed to be loosely based upon Sanderson Miller, and there are scenes and characteristics which are thought to be very much of Radway, where Fielding was a frequent and welcome visitor.

The trees upon the hillside were planted by William Pitt (the Elder) First Lord Chatham, again in a kind of retrospective commemoration of the Edgehill fight.

Miller, having decided that follies were the thing, went further and built some faintly ecclesiastical fortified 'ruins' near the tower. They abutted the road and there are still pictures extant showing them, ivy clad and crumbling. Sadly, these are long since disappeared, and the Radway Tower is now a public house.

Miller's eccentricity increased with age, and towards the end of his life he fell out with those who had once been his friends. He had to be confined in the house of a doctor and looked after until his death. He was collecting material for a great treatise upon architecture, urged on in this project by Horace Walpole, who is said to have admired his style. But the work never came to fruition.

Sanderson Miller's grandson, Lieutenant-Colonel F.S. Miller, commanded the Iniskilling Dragoons at the Battle of Waterloo. He was a gallant and brave soldier, and was severely wounded. But he survived, and was made Companion of the Bath.

Another distinguished soldier happened to be staying at Radway Grange at the outbreak of the First World War. Field Marshall Earl Haig (as he later became) was called to London urgently by telegram, and set off in a motor car on 2nd August 1914. But motor cars being what they were in 1914, and Sun Rising Hill being what it still is, the car couldn't make the steep, almost vertical gradient. The Field Marshall fumed and fretted, for he had to catch the London train from Banbury. There was only one possible way. The car was rolled backward down Sun Rising Hill, turned around, and the chauffeur *reversed* all the way up to the top! The Field Marshall caught his train.

The lychgate outside the church serves as a memorial to those who fell in the First World War, and to that other more famous 'local', the Field Marshall, who died in 1928.

Ratley

Approached from the top of the Edgehill escarpment, Ratley prides itself on being both the oldest and the highest village in Warwickshire. High it certainly is, some 600 ft above sea level, and with superb views right across the Oxfordshire plateau, just across the invisible county boundary.

The village is in the form of a long low loop, and it does show that our ancestors certainly knew how to build, for all the houses, built of the yellow ochre ironstone quarried in these parts, look as if they have grown out of the earth, and they shelter each other. The different levels, irregularities of walls and roof lines, the varying window shapes, and fertile gardens make this main village street a true delight.

Close by are the remains of Nadbury Camp, an ancient earthwork, cut through now by a busy road and much damaged in recent years by ploughing. It seems our forbears liked to have their homes up high as well, and thus obtain a good view of any possible marauders.

The older inhabitants of Ratley can remember how in the Second World War they stood upon the top of their hill and watched the fires of both Coventry and Birmingham, as those cities were ruthlessly bombed by the Luftwaffe. One of the German bombers flew low over Ratley, scattering bits of flaming fuselage as it thundered past to nose dive into the hillside, and when daylight dawned the bloodstained maps from the pilot's cockpit were found blowing around the main street.

They were close to another war in Ratley too, for just to the north, no more than a stone's throw, they look down upon the plain where the battle of Edgehill was fought. Many soldiers who made their way to Ratley in the aftermath are buried in a mass grave beneath mounds behind the church. Within living memory bones have sometimes worked their way up to the surface, and have had to be reverently reburied. No one knows who these men were, or from whence they came.

The church is dedicated to St Peter ad Vincula (St Peter in Chains). It stands in a clearing facing the village green, and has managed to escape the worst excesses of the earnest restorer. There are a few brass memorial plates, one of which is worthy of attention, for upon it is a monumental mistake. It refers to the heiress of Simon Bury, who married into the Lewis family. It tells us that she died on 14th February, Anno Domini 1696 aged (Ae tat suoe) 1697. I think the poor brass engraver was trying to get it finished before knocking off on the Friday before a Bank holiday!

On the memorial to those who served in the First World War, there are 17 men with the surname 'England', four of whom laid down their lives. The family is still in Ratley, and others of that name served in the Second World War.

In the chancel is a memorial tablet to the Earl of Jersey, who is not buried at Ratley, but at Middleton Stoney, and thereby hangs a tale! In the neighbouring parish of Upton, there is a beautiful 18th century mansion, Upton House, now in the care of the National Trust. Upton House has had many owners, and all of them improved it in their own fashion. It was almost entirely rebuilt in the 1920s. There is parkland surrounding it, and its owners have also owned land and houses within Ratley.

In 1757, Upton House came into the ownership of Mr Francis Child, a very rich banker. Mr Child had an only daughter of whom he was very fond, and for whom he intended great things. He also had a friend, the young Earl of Westmorland, of that slightly impoverished family.

One night at dinner, the Earl nonchalantly asked his host, 'What would you do if you were in love with a young lady, and could not marry her because her father would not give his consent?'

Unsuspectingly, Mr Child laughingly answered, 'I shouldn't take 'No' for an answer. Indeed, I should run off with her'.

A few days later Mr Child discovered his advice had been faithfully followed and the Earl of Westmorland had run off with his only daughter. Irate, he pursued the couple all the way to Gretna Green, but arrived too late to prevent the marriage. He had his revenge, although I doubt it could have been sweet. He swore that none of his money should go towards propping up the less than well-to-do Westmorlands, and accordingly he left all his property in Upton and in Ratley to his daughter's second surviving child, Lady Sarah Fane, who married George, 5th Earl of Jersey, and so brought Ratley, Upton and all else to that family. When the Jerseys inherited Upton, there was a debate about whether they should live there, but they decided against it because the roads were almost always so bad as to be impassable.

Later, Upton House came into the possession of Mr Morant Gale, a passionate sportsman, who owned sugar plantations in the West Indies. He brought over one of his men, Negro Molyneux, a pugilist, to fight the famous Tom Cribb. Molyneux was a notable fighter, but Cribb was the best. Accordingly, an illegal bout was fixed up in a remote and lonely spot near Upton, when the rector and any of those others who might have called in the law, were known to be away from home.

Tom Cribb and Negro Molyneux fought bare knuckled on 23rd December 1810, in this remote and isolated spot, with a crowd of gamblers, punters and sportsmen watching and betting. Tom Cribb won the fight, and Mr Morant Gale lost quite a parcel of money, having laid his bets on Molyneux.

Rowington

Rowington, called Rochintone in the old Domesday survey because it stands upon rocky ground, is not so much a village in the accepted sense of the word as a scattering of groups of buildings, some of them very beautiful. Once it stood well within the Forest of Arden, and indeed is still fairly well wooded, although what time and development left, the dread Dutch elm disease took care of. Yet there are still narrow and leafy lanes, typical of old Warwickshire, and there is the wonderful church of St Lawrence towering high above you on a hill where the road bends sharply.

The main road is a leafy lane no more though. It is the main B4439 carrying fast traffic to Warwick, and further depredations are caused by the close proximity of the new M40 motorway.

Rowington's history stretches back to the time of the Saxons. It was sometime during the reign of Henry I (1068-1135) that the Abbot of Reading founded a small priory of Cistercian nuns here. The priory seems to have been well conducted, and a few remnants of its old buildings still remain, although not readily recognisable. However, in 1350 Bishop Thoresby of Worcester issued an order for the removal of certain secular persons from this house because of 'ill fame' attaching to the nuns. It would seem these secular persons, whoever they may have been, were giving the place a bad name.

By 1536 when Henry VIII began the Dissolution, there were only four nuns, a prioress and eight dependents left there. The last abbess was Margaret Wigston, and the site and lands occupied by the priory were sold to William Wigston, son of the last high steward at the priory. It seems obvious that William and Margaret were related, although exactly how is not known. At least we may assume the last abbess was not sent forth to wander in a hostile world as so many were.

When Henry VIII married his sixth and last wife, Katherine

Parr in 1544 he gave her Rowington as part of her marriage jointure, but it is doubtful if this lady ever saw it.

In a village of interesting houses, perhaps the one that attracts most attention is Shakespeare Hall and long have experts vied with each other over the stories attaching to it. There was a branch of the Shakespeare family at Rowington, that much is certain. The name first appears in the parish registers in 1485, and there are no less than four William Shakespeares recorded between 1560 and 1614. Some scholars claim that the Thomas Shakespeare who lived in the house in 'our' Will's time was in fact his uncle, elder brother to his father, John. It might only be a coincidence that this Thomas had a son, John, who was apprenticed to William Jaggard, commonly called the 'pirate publisher' who first published *The Passionate Pilgrim*, a collection of 21 poems attributed to William Shakespeare. Five certainly were by the Bard, but the others undoubtedly were not, and the publisher removed his name from the volume. Jaggard also published the First Folio.

Many believe that William Shakespeare visited his relatives at Rowington, which is only about twelve miles from Stratford. It is said he went to church with them, either at Rowington or at nearby Baddesley Clinton, and may well have roamed around Hay Wood, singing a brief 'Hey Nonny' while he pondered on the lines he needed for *As You Like It*. In his time there must have been quite a lot of the old forest left.

It seems appropriate that to Rowington (Rochintone, rocky) in 1853 should come a vicar who was to remain for 44 years, whose name became synonymous with the study of many aspects of natural history, but particularly geology.

Peter Bellinger Brodie was born in London in 1815, son of a successful barrister. As a youngster he spent as much of his spare time as he could in the Museum of Natural History at the Royal College of Surgeons, and so enthusiastic was he that the Curator of the College proposed him as a Fellow of the Geological Society at the relatively tender age of 19, the youngest-ever Fellow. He went to Emmanuel College, Cambridge, where in 1838 he read his first paper to the Cambridge Philosophical Society with the exceedingly long title of 'Notes on the

Occurrence of Land and Freshwater Shells with Bones of some Extinct Animals in the Gravel near Cambridge'. It was well received. But meanwhile he had his more formal studies to pursue, and in that same year he was ordained deacon.

His first clerical appointment was as curate at Wylye in Wiltshire, where he discovered the fossilized remains of a genus of shellfish hitherto unknown to the scientific world, and this was later named after him *Archaeoniscus brodiei*. In 1839 he was ordained priest.

Then came other livings in Buckinghamshire and in Gloucestershire before he came to Rowington in 1853. After the richly fossilized rocks of the Cotswolds, Rowington may not have been too inspiring, but here Rev Peter Brodie was to remain until his death, and here he was to produce some of his best work.

He immediately joined the Warwickshire Natural History and Archaeological Society, and was elected honorary Curator of Geology. He was a tireless collector, and his work greatly enhanced the collections of the Society which are now displayed in the Market Hall Museum in Warwick. His own personal collection numbered some 25,000 specimens, and the British Museum purchased many of these.

Perhaps his greatest triumph came in 1887 when he was awarded the prestigious Murchison Medal from the Geological Society of London for his outstanding contributions, and in his reply at the presentation ceremony he hints at the great conflict in his life between his pastoral work and his passionate interest in geology. He explained to the society that he had only been able to work in the natural sciences during his hours of leisure, and the distance from London had precluded him from attending as many meetings of the Society, of which he had been a member for the past 53 years, as he would have wished.

He died at Rowington, aged 82, on 1st November 1897 and the work he left behind included a superb collection of scientifically important fossils and more than a hundred published papers on a wide range of natural history subjects. He achieved an enviable reputation among all those connected with geology and his contribution to greater knowledge in that field is incalculable.

He was described as a 'Dear old man, who loved God's world, children, animals and nature'. There can be few better epitaphs. A bust of this reverend gentleman stands in the Market Place Museum, from which we see him as rather tall, craggy browed, with a large straight nose and square beard. Very much the archetypal Victorian parson.

It is strange how many Victorian parsons throughout Warwickshire, and probably elsewhere, did such sterling work in the field of natural history. It can only be supposed that when they had but one parish to serve they did at least have some time to spare. Certainly, had it not been for the Victorian parson, riding the leafy lanes, mile after mile on a heavy sit-up-and-beg bicycle, we should have been denied much of our present knowledge, and much that has interested subsequent generations might have been lost for all time.

Ryton-on-Dunsmore

Ryton-on-Dunsmore now finds itself on the outskirts of Coventry, and as such could scarcely be called hidden, although it is often visited because of the interesting organic gardening establishment featured on television.

However, the main A45 leaving Ryton crosses Dunsmore Heath and, near Knightlow Hill is the scene of one of the most extraordinary ghost stories in the county. We have our fair share of black dogs, grey ladies and monks, but this haunting takes the form of a ghost lorry.

At the time of the hauntings, this stretch of road was much narrower, curving and tree-fringed. It was not until later that it became the much trafficked highway it is now. Many people saw, or thought they saw, the spectral lorry and tales abounded. The local police constable lived in a house quite close to this particular stretch of road, and in the course of his duties he heard many times of the ghost vehicle, but not being a superstitious man he tended to disregard them.

It was a fairly dangerous stretch of road, and there were several accidents. Upon many occasions, the constable helping a driver from the wreckage heard of 'a big lorry coming straight at me' but was frankly sceptical. That is until one dark night in the 1950s, when he had cause to change his mind.

It was towards the end of November, and a dreadful night, with the worst of weather conditions. Freezing fog which reduced visibility to a desperate level, flurries of snow that drove against windscreens, and an icy road surface. The inevitable happened. Along this stretch of road came a lorry, which misjudged the curve, skidded, slewed round, and turned over on its side. Within minutes a car had run right into the crashed vehicle. The two vehicles, a mass of intermeshed metal, completely blocked the road, and it was not long before they were joined by further vehicles, who because of the weather conditions came round the curve and were unable to stop in time.

It was a nightmare, and the local constable was desperately trying to tackle it single handed whilst he waited for help to arrive. His most urgent task was to find a way of warning oncoming vehicles so that they too would not crash and add to the wreckage. He gathered together a few of the drivers, thankfully uninjured, and set them pulling down brush from the hedgerow. This was piled into the middle of the road and set ablaze as a bonfire beacon, and it worked, for as cars approached they saw the flames and slowed to a halt.

The constable and his helpers breathed an all too brief sigh of relief, when suddenly one of the men shouted 'Look out. Here comes another . . .'. The constable looked, and to his total disbelief he saw a large lorry, dark in colour, its back covered with tarpaulins, coming towards them at great speed with all its lights blazing.

The constable and the other men moved forward, unable to credit that the driver of the lorry could not see the flames. The vehicle did not slacken speed at all, and as they watched, it drove straight through the flames of the fire. But . . . the wood fire didn't move, and the yellow flames showed clearly through the sides of the lorry. As the vehicle hurtled on its way, it also passed through the group of men, who leapt back out of the way. But the constable and the men saw each other clearly *through* the seemingly solid sides of the lorry.

Aghast and terrified, they all waited to hear the crash as the lorry headed towards the pile of metal blocking the road. They ran towards the spot, waiting for the scream of brakes. But they heard nothing. It never happened. The pile of bent metal remained stationary, untouched. There was no sign of the speeding lorry, not even a brief glimpse of its tail lights in the darkness of the night.

It passed through the flames, passed entirely through a group of shaken men, and passed through a pile of crashed wreckage, and was no more. And at least six ordinary, somewhat sceptical, honest citizens witnessed it.

Stoneleigh

Say the word 'Stoneleigh' and everyone immediately thinks of the Royal Agricultural Show ground, quite understandably. Although hundreds of thousands visit this every year, few people penetrate as far as the village of Stoneleigh itself; a picture book village of black and white timbered cottages. Here and there, it is true, today's architecture has intruded, but the village despite its close proximity to the large city of Coventry remains singularly and pleasingly unspoiled.

It is very close to Stoneleigh Abbey, long the home of the Leigh family, wherein their distant relation, Jane Austen, often stayed. Stoneleigh was a royal manor even before the days of William the Conqueror. It was a place of some importance and the old Hundred Court was held on what is now called Motslow Hill, Motslow deriving from 'moot' or meeting place.

Eight centuries ago Cistercian monks founded Stoneleigh Abbey, and lived out their diligent lives in their pleasant woodland home, for Stoneleigh in their day was well hidden within the Forest of Arden. However in 1365 they complained of their abbot, Thomas de Pipe, who was selling off lands belonging to the abbey in order to support his paramour, Isabell Beushale. Imagine their further consternation, therefore, when upon investigation it was discovered that the abbot and Isabell had, in their unblessed and illicit union, produced more children than there were monks within the abbey.

The abbey suffered the fate of all such religious houses at the Dissolution, and came into the hands of the Suffolk family, who thus brought down upon their heads the ancient curse that those unwise enough to use Church property for their own personal gain come to no good end. Although the Duke of Suffolk had two sons when he acquired the abbey, they died childless and the direct line came to an end.

Eventually, Sir Thomas Leigh, Lord Mayor of London, acquired Stoneleigh. He it was who rode be-plumed before Queen Elizabeth I on the way to her Coronation. His wife was Dame Alice Leigh, but it was their daughter, also Alice Leigh, whose reputation as a benefactress spread throughout the area. This good lady endowed almshouses, left bequests, gave money, founded charities and is remembered in many and diverse places.

The poor lady herself didn't have too easy a time of it. She was born in 1578 and ultimately married the dashing Robert Dudley, son of the Earl of Leicester and his second wife, Lady Sheffield. Four daughters were born to Robert Dudley and Alice Leigh, and they all lived at Kenilworth Castle while Robert Dudley sought to establish his claim to his father's estates and titles.

There was a problem because Leicester's marriage to Lady Sheffield had been a secret one, and Robert Dudley had to prove the legitimacy of his birth. He was impeded in this by his father's third wife, Lettice, once widow of Walter Devereaux, Earl of Essex. If Robert had been declared legitimate, this would have meant that her own marriage to his father was bigamous.

When Robert Dudley finally lost his case, was declared illegitimate and could not inherit from his father, he went off in a huff to tour Italy, accompanied by a page boy, leaving Alice Leigh at home to bring up their daughters. He never returned from Italy; obviously a chip off the old block, for the page boy, his constant companion, turned out to be none other than Elizabeth Southwell once lady in waiting to Queen Elizabeth. They set up house together, and their union produced twelve children. The Emperor of Italy created Dudley a Duke of the Holy Roman Empire, with the titles of Earl of Warwick and Duke of Northumberland.

Alice Leigh was left to get on with her ruined life as best she might. She had a large estate and a large fortune to administer, and whether she ever thought bitterly of her rake of a husband, or whether she wished he would return, no one ever knew. She devoted herself to many good works, and espoused the cause of King Charles I who in 1645 created her a duchess in her own right, the first and only woman ever to achieve this great honour.

Alice, Duchess Dudley, lived to be 90 years of age, dying in January 1669. There is a fine marble tomb in the little church at Stoneleigh, with effigies of Alice and her daughter, sculpted by Nicholas Stone. She reclines on the upper tier, while below her lies the daughter who died some 48 years before her mother. So many are the good works of this great lady, who bore all her sorrows with remarkable fortitude and great dignity, that she is formally remembered in church at Stoneleigh every Whitsunday.

An older and much stranger effigy rests within the porch of the church. It was brought in from the churchyard, but not before centuries of wind and weather had polished it almost to obliteration. It is a figure of a woman holding what seems to be an infant. No one has ever discovered the true story, but in 1637, the vicar of Stoneleigh, Edward Maunsell, wrote:

> 'there is a tradition among the comm people of stoneley yt anty there was a goodly house standing upon the hill called Motstow Hill on the south pt of the church which was the habitacion of a knight who going to the warrs left his lady gt wt childe and upon the news that he was slayne she ript up her own belly and was buried therefore upon the north side of the church in ye churchyard under a stone whereupon is portraied the figure of a woman and a child wh remaynes to this daye . . . '.

And this would seem to be the lady whose husband was 'slayne' in some war or other, and who could not face life without him. Later, much later, she was brought into the shelter of the church, the shelter that was denied her upon her death by her own hand. Poor soul, she was obviously not made of such stern stuff as Alice Leigh.

Sutton Under Brailes

◣ Deep in the south, the lush green part of Warwickshire, nudging the Cotswolds, this small and lovely village was referred to as the 'South Farm' in the Domesday survey. The 'under Brailes' part of its name comes from the fact that it lies snugly tucked under Brailes Hill, the second highest point in the county. Sutton brook runs across one corner of the parish, sometimes called the 'wash brook' wherein sheep were dipped a century or so ago. Sutton brook joins itself on to the quiet river Stour, and Sutton Mill still stands, almost certainly upon the same site as the original mill mentioned in Domesday. This one no longer grinds corn, though.

There are no major roads through Sutton under Brailes; merely a slight criss-crossing of narrow ways, and the soft-coloured stone houses are irregularly set upon all four sides of a huge village green.

Mature and lofty trees bedecked this green at one time, but the years and disease took their toll and the great giants are no more. The Great Elm of Sutton, 150 ft high, came down in 1967, and in 1971 Dutch Elm disease spread rapidly through the county causing the loss of 900,000 elms, often referred to as the 'Warwickshire Weed', in less than ten years. There has been replanting at Sutton under Brailes, but the Great Elm is lamented yet. A vast, gnarled, knotted old bole remains upon one side of the green; stunted and topless, a reminder of past grandeur, and now used mostly to stick up posters and notices.

The church of St Thomas a Becket is tucked away in a corner, and is a pleasant, ancient and unpretentious building. But it does have a notable peal of five bells, cast by the brothers

William and Robert Corin 1701, and thought to be of outstanding historical interest. They are the second earliest Cor ring in the country, and are unique in that they are extensively ornamented, with arabesque borders, floral motifs, the Royal coat of arms, angels, cherubs and the Magi.

One of the bells still bears the name of Henry Croft, who was once churchwarden at Sutton, and the Croft family is of great importance in the history of this part of Warwickshire. It really began when Sir John de Croft married Janet, daughter of the Prince of Wales, Owain Glendower, round about the year 1400. Two of their grandsons served as squires to the Duke of York's sons at Ludlow Castle, and when one of these young princes became Edward IV, the Croft family fortunes were on the up-and-up. Richard Croft became lord of the manor of Chipping Norton, about eight miles away from Sutton under Brailes in Oxfordshire, and during the first half of the 16th century members of the Croft family moved into Sutton under Brailes, where they remained for some seven generations, living in a lovely old farmhouse known as the Townend House. They married into various notable local families, always improving their social standing and their fortunes. Sixteen members of this Croft family were students at Oxford, and there is no doubt at all that they were learned and cultured people.

William Croft, born in 1678, was to become perhaps the most illustrious of his family. William became a composer of church music, sharing the Chapel Royal with Jeremiah Clarke (who composed the *Trumpet Voluntary*) and working with Henry Purcell. William Croft has been described as a gentle man, and it is thought that his childhood in the lush green pastures of Warwickshire inspired him so successfully to create his music.

He was certainly prolific. His *Musica Sacra* was 30 anthems, and among his many admirers was John Wesley, who was deeply moved after hearing *Out of the Deep Have I called to Thee*. Croft wrote anthems for the funeral of Queen Anne, and the music for the Coronations of George I and II. He also wrote the music for the State Burial Service, which is still in use today. But the piece of music by which he is best known throughout all village churches is quite simply that much loved old hymn *O*

God Our Help in Ages Past. William Croft died in 1727, at the age of 50, and is buried with honour in Westminster Abbey.

The only trace of the Croft family at Sutton under Brailes now is the bell bearing Henry's name. The bells were in great danger in 1982, but the tiny village of Sutton took only 18 months to work diligently and raise the £10,000 necessary to carry out the extensive work needed. The bells are now safe and 'sound' again.

Tredington

The older part of this village, lying just a couple of miles north of Shipston-on-Stour, is probably the mostphotographed of all Warwickshire villages, and with some justification, for it is beautiful. Its houses and cottages of varying shapes, sizes and periods, cluster around a small village green, and its thatch and roses have long been a delight to tourists.

The village is of Saxon origin, and until 1931 formed an island of Gloucestershire within Warwickshire. The old Oxford Turnpike ran across the top end of the green, and at the beginning of the last century mail coaches ran daily. The 'Day Coach' ran from Birmingham to Oxford, and went through Tredington at precisely 3 pm. The *Paul Pry* went in the opposite direction. The *Oxonion*; the *Union*; the *Prince of Wales* and the *Britannia* ran on alternate days to London via Tredington, so the Turnpike was busy even then. It has now become the main A34 and is even busier, for it cuts the village cleanly in two, separating the older part from more recently built houses on the opposite side of the road.

The area used to belong to Wulstan, Bishop of Worcester, and it is believed that it was he who built the original church in AD 961. The building was altered early in the 14th century and dedicated to St Gregory, but it was not until the 19th century that Saxon remains were discovered below its enormous 15th century spire which rises to some 200 ft or so, and completely dominates the surrounding landscape.

Tredington is unique within our County for having a 'Peculiar

Court' in that it was not subject to the ordinary rule of the presiding Bishop. The old rectors were, in effect, Lords of the Parish, and the records of the goings-on of the Peculiar Court are still in existence. They mostly concern various residents being brought to book for working on Sundays, or not sending their children to church, or for allowing gatherings of Non-Conformists. There were also charges like 'knowingly entertaining fornicators and incontinents' in which case the rector dismissed the offender with a caution.

The church had many treasures, which included two superb silver flagons dating from 1638. Several years ago there was much controversy, reported in the press, when it endeavoured to sell these. After a long legal battle in the Court of Arches, the sale was eventually allowed. The flagons were bought by a Portugese collector of English silver, and some of the money was used to carry out more restoration to the church, which had already undergone extensive restoration in 1899. The antique flagons were replaced with modern ones. But at the time quite a lot of people were opposed to the sale of such irreplaceable church property.

The people of Tredington have not always been law-abiding. In 1404 tenants of Tredington marched to Shipston-on-Stour, and started a riot, all about the heriot tax. This, in effect, meant that the best beast from the farm went to the Lord of the Manor upon the death of the tenant of the farm. The riot settled nothing, but the Abbot of Winchcombe decided that the Priory should receive the best beast, and the parson of the parish the next best.

Some five years later in 1409, the parson of Tredington, Richard Wych, who was also a farmer, together with several of his friends, broke into the manor house, and carried off windows with their fastenings. They broke into the dovecote and stole the doves, and assaulted the servants. It seems the people of Tredington enjoyed a bit of a fight now and again, and Richard Wych was letting the Bishop know he wasn't pleased at being turned off his farm.

Tredington did give birth to one notable. Admiral Sir Charles Hyde Parker born here on 1st February 1713, while his father was Rector. He was to become Commander of the British fleet at the Battle of Copenhagen, and it is said he it was who issued the signal to which Nelson turned a blind eye.

His naval career was one of disaster. The explanation he gave to King George II when he made such a mess of things in the American States was simple 'Sir you have need of younger men and newer ships . . .'. However, his own ventures proved extremely profitable. On one occasion he captured the return ship from Manila to Acapulco, which yielded him a cool £30,000. And when he was in the Leeward Islands, he captured a whole convoy of twenty ships, and accounted for many more including sloops of war and three frigates. There are memorials to Sir Hyde Parker's family in Tredington church.

Tredington has had its due and proper share of witches, like most other Warwickshire villages, the most famous witch being Betty Lofs, who seems to have perpetually caused trouble . When not invited to a party, which she thought she was justly entitled to attend, she turned up in the guise of a cat, but was stuck through the paw by a pitchfork. The cat disappeared, and sure enough, the following morning Betty was seen with her right hand bandaged! She apparently took against one of her neighbours, a man called Lambley. He couldn't get his fire to draw, his beer to ferment, nor his butter to 'come' all on account of Betty. So he did the decent thing and gave her a present of free milk every week. From that time on he had no trouble.

Another Tredington witch, also called Betty, used to be seen sitting in a withy tree near the churchyard, smoking an old clay pipe. Even after her death, local people still declared they could see her there.

Tredington used to enjoy a Wakes Day, held on 28th June, St Agatha's Day, and apart from the usual wheelbarrow and sack races, wrestling, bowling and all night dancing, the great feature was the parade of chimney sweeps carrying garlands. It would appear a good time was had by all. But alas Tredington Wake is gone, along with many others, a regular event in Warwickshire villages, and now replaced with a much more decorous Fete.

Upper & Lower Shuckburgh

Almost on the borders of Northamptonshire, Lower Shuckburgh sits upon the side of the main Daventry Road, whilst the deserted medieval village of Upper Shuckburgh is about a mile further on.

No trace remains of this old village, but Shuckburgh Hall, the home of the family since the 11th century, looms out from amid the trees on Beacon Hill, the 'haunt of goblins'. On rising ground in the gently rolling acres is the church of St John in the Wilderness, which belonged at one time to the nuns of Wroxall and went, like so many others, in the Dissolution.

The Hall and church are surrounded by a private deer park, with a herd of pure bred fallow deer, beautiful creatures, scuttering gracefully among the trees. The origins of the Shuckburgh herd go back centuries. They were here when that intrepid traveller, Celia Fiennes, visited the house in 1697. She wrote of their tameness, and how they came right up to the house.

Celia Fiennes was on her way from Warwick to Daventry, and both the party and their horses were fatigued. 'We could have no entertainment', she says. It seems that Lady Shuckburgh (or as Miss Fiennes puts it, 'Shugberry') passed by in her coach, and noticed the distress of the travellers. When she got home, she sent her husband, Sir Charles, to go and meet the party and offer them hospitality.

Miss Fiennes describes the house as 'well furnished tho not very rich, but in generall all things were very well as any Private Gentleman . . .'. She relates how Sir Charles ordered one of his daughters to 'dig up a curiosity' for his guest. This was a fossil shaped very like an heraldic five-point star, and referred to in the area as an 'Arms' because of its resemblance to the heraldic 'mullet'. They were plentiful upon Beacon Hill, we are told.

Celia Fiennes' host, Sir Charles, was the grandson of probably the most notable of the Shuckburghs, Squire Richard. Richard was a countryman, who lived the quiet life of a man of his station and troubled himself little about affairs of state. On 22nd October 1642, King Charles I was preparing for Edgehill, and

Church of St John in the Wilderness, Upper Shuckburgh

his army was gathering. The King noticed a gentleman out hunting, with an excellent pack of hounds. The King, with the cares of state lying heavy upon his shoulders, asked his officers 'Who is that gentleman with so few cares that he can hunt, while I must fight for my Crown and dignity?' Upon being told that it was Mr Richard Shuckburgh, the King asked that he be brought to him.

Richard Shuckburgh knew nothing of the war, and didn't even know it was happening! In rural Warwickshire, he had simply gone about his own business. Upon meeting his King, he was complimented upon his hounds, a pack of some note, and the King said he wished he could have joined him in so carefree a sport. Richard Shuckburgh promptly rode back to his home, gathered up as many of his tenants and servants as he could, and returned with them to Edgehill to fight at his King's side. For his valour upon the field of battle, he was knighted.

After the taking of Banbury Castle, and when the King had left and was on his way to Oxford, Shuckburgh returned home and fortified his house. He was attacked by Parliamentarian forces on top of Shuckburgh Hill, where he and his tenants put up a good fight. Sir Richard fell, severely wounded, was taken prisoner and lodged in Kenilworth Castle for a long time.

In the skirmish the church of St John was damaged, but many of the memorials and monuments to past Shuckburghs were saved. Inside the church is a fine memorial bust to Sir Richard, showing him with the pointed beard so fashionable in his day. It is the only signed work in the country by Peter Bennier, sculptor to King Charles II. Sir Richard died in 1656, at the age of 60, and his son John served the second King Charles as faithfully as his father had served the first.

The old timbered house visited by Celia Fiennes is now hidden by a Victorian stucco front, built when the house was made over in the more fashionable tastes of 1844.

There is an amusing correspondence still in existence, between Lady Shuckburgh and Lady Seymour, a famous beauty of her day. Lady Seymour, recently voted Queen of Beauty, wrote to Lady Shuckburgh asking for a 'character' for one Mary Steadman, a kitchen maid in the Shuckburgh establishment. Lady Shuckburgh replied that kitchen maids were beneath her notice, and that she kept a cook and a housekeeper to deal with such things. Enquiries should therefore be addressed to them. She knew nothing of the merits or abilities of under servants, but she personally doubted if Mary Steadman was capable of cooking anything except for the servant's hall.

Lady Seymour tartly replied that her children could not be kept without their dinners just because Lady Shuckburgh thought a knowledge of the details of her establishment beneath her; would she please therefore instruct her housekeeper to write the girl a character.

The housekeeper, a Mrs Elizabeth Couch, replied to Lady Seymour that Lady Shuckburgh considered the vulgarity of her letter 'beneath contempt' although, as she puts it 'it might be characteristic of the Sheridans (Lady Seymour's family) to be coarse, vulgar and witty'. She suggested that Lady Seymour might have been 'born in a garrett and bred in a kitchen'. As Mary Steadman informed her, Mrs Couch, that she would be required to cook a mutton chop, she supposed that either Mary Steadman 'or any other scullion' would be fully equal to the establishment of the 'Queen of Beauty'.

We don't know whether Mary Steadman got taken on in the

establishment of the Queen of Beauty (Lady Seymour) or whether she got her wrist slapped and remained a scullion in the Shuckburgh kitchen.

Lower Shuckburgh, a mere handful of cottages, is dominated by its 'new' church, built in 1864. It shows signs of Eastern influence, dictated by George Shuckburgh when he returned from the Crimean War.

Another Shuckburgh who brought foreign ideas back from war service was Major Henry James, who served in the Afghan Wars. He built four estate cottages at Lower Shuckburgh, and they each bear his initials 'H.J.S.' but he decided to name them after the campaigns in which he fought, namely Joaki, Cabul, Gundamuck and Nowshera. A rather nice notion, but one cannot help but wonder how the tenants took to living in a cottage with what was, to them, a singularly outlandish name.

Wappenbury

Very much 'hidden' Warwickshire, for truly a search has to be made before you eventually arrive at the centre of this green, quiet, oasis of a village.

And yet it does not appear to have always been so. Wappenbury is an ancient settlement, and its name comes from 'Wappa's burgh'. Here Wappa and his family, plus presumably many others, had an extensive burgh in the form of an Iron Age embankment, now scheduled as an ancient monument. In the centre of it stands the present village, not very far from the long straight Roman road, the Fosse Way.

The earthworks at Wappenbury are believed to be the largest of their type throughout the Midlands, and there have been several careful and organised expert excavations which have yielded many interesting objects. Four kilns were found, dating from around AD 350, together with examples of the grey ware which they turned out, and of which the Romans, certainly those around Warwickshire, seem to have been especially fond.

In the 13th century, Wappenbury was overrun by the plague. Some 200 villagers died, and so we may assume that it must have been much larger than at present. For now it has nothing like so many residents.

The church of St John suffered from over restoration, as indeed did many churches. It seems that having made some money in Midlands manufacture, nothing would satisfy the Victorians other than to spend it upon 'restoring' their local church! There is a mural tablet inside the church which makes for quite quaint reading:

> A lingering sickness did me seize
> And no physician could me ease
> I fought for help but all in vain
> Until the Lord did ease my pain.

There is, however, one of a more recent date, very much to the point, with a disconsolate woman sitting in a cornfield. This is to William Umbers, whom we are told was a 'zealous and scientific agriculturalist, and an uncompromising advocate of every public measure which he considered calculated to foster the production and industry of this country'. He died aged 52 on 2nd July 1849. His memorial certainly makes him sound fierce.

Warmington

This is one of Warwickshire's truly picture book villages; the kind that appears on calendars and the lids of biscuit tins, for its heart and core has changed but little, and it is well tucked away so that to get to it it is necessary to leave the beaten track and take to the lanes.

The wide village green slopes and curves gracefully towards the village pond wherein ducks gleefully disport themselves, probably the direct descendants of the ducks that have always lived upon Warmington pond. The houses, different shapes, different sizes, and all venerable, surround the green, holding themselves slightly aloof, their yellowish brown stone walls holding firmly to the secrets of centuries, their gardens vibrant with blossom, and their many-paned windows glinting in the sun.

Upon a jutting rocky outcrop above the village stands the church of St Michael. Close behind it, and away from the village, runs the main A41 rising sharply and curving upwards from the lowlands of Warwickshire to the high plateau of Oxfordshire. Traffic hurtles past at a great rate, and the ancient church shakes with its roar. It is far better to approach it from the village down below, although to do so you need to climb a long pine-shaded pathway, where violets grow beneath the trees, and to stagger up some 50 odd steps.

Why the parish church should have been built so high and in such a comparatively inaccessible place is a bit of a mystery. The monks of Preaux (Normandy) had a cell down in the village and legend has it that it was decided to build the church down there. However, mysterious elements decreed otherwise. After each day's work, fairies came along in the night and removed stone after stone, so that the building work made no progress whatsoever. As soon as it was decided to build the church high upon the rock, the fairies stopped playing tricks and the work went ahead unhindered.

Warmington village pond

The church has stood here, dominating and keeping guard over the village for the past 700 years, and its tower, silhouetted against the skyline has been a landmark since the year 1300. It may have been the sight of this that made many of those escaping from the Battle of Edgehill, just a few miles off, make their way towards Warmington for help and comfort. Within the pine-shaded churchyard, among many ancient and leaning stones, is a memorial to Captain Alexander Gourdin, a Scotsman, who died here of his wounds. It seems that others were helped too, for the parish records reveal:

'The Battell was fought by our Sovraine Lord King Charles and the earle of Essex the three and twentieth day of October, being Sabbeath Day, Ano Dom 1642, partely between Radwaie (Radway) and Kington (Kineton). Richard Sauner, captaine of a Footte Companie, a gentleman of Worcestershier, was buried in Warmington Churchyard the four and twentieth day of October Ano Dom 1642. Alexander Gourdin, a Scotsman, was buried the five and twentieth day of October Ano Dom 1642 ut supra. Also seven others were buried in Warmington Churchyard whose names I know not, and it is reported that one or two more were buried within the fields and windes of Warmington aforesaid . . .'.

The only marked grave is that of the Scot, Alexander Gourdin, and one is left wondering why Richard Sauner, the 'gentleman of Worcestershier' does not have one, or whether all the others were buried together. Many of the wounded must have limped and crawled their desperate way to Warmington, and the villagers must have cared for many of them, and then decently buried those who did not survive.

At some stage, there was an anchorite cell on the south-west side of the church. Who the anchorite was, we know not, except that she apparently spent her entire life in devotions in that tiny room, seeing nothing but the high altar of the church through a narrow slit. Later, this tiny room was used as a sleeping chamber for a clergyman, who also acted as a kind of caretaker. Local legend has it that the little room is haunted, and there are times when a sweet clear voice is heard coming from within.

Warwick

One could hardly call the St John's House Museum in the town of Warwick 'hidden' but in one dark corner of it is a fascinating story.

Upstairs St John's House is devoted to the history of the Royal Warwickshire regiment, with medals, uniforms, stories, ephemera, battle honours, and everything else that one would expect of a military museum. Tucked away in one corner is the story of Hannah Snell.

Hannah was born in Friar Street, Worcester, in 1723. We don't know what she looked like, for there is no likeness of her. But in 1745, at the age of 22 years, Hannah came to Coventry and enlisted in the 6th Regiment, using the name James Grey.

She marched with the regiment to Carlisle, but she hadn't been long there when for some reason or other, she upset the sergeant, and was sentenced to receive 500 lashes. Even then, no one tumbled to her secret. After receiving this punishment, she deserted. Quite a natural reaction I should think, and she hied herself down to Portsmouth where she promptly enlisted in the Marines. It was not long before Hannah Snell set sail for the East Indies.

She was fighting at the Siege of Pondicherry in 1748, and it seems was right there in the front line, for she was severely wounded. She had twelve shot wounds, eleven in her legs and one in her groin. She was taken to the surgeons just like any other soldier, and was treated for her wounds. Goodness knows how, but she still managed to keep her secret. You really would have thought the surgeons would have noticed something! However, Hannah made a good recovery.

She returned to England in 1750, and only then did she reveal her secret, that she was a woman and had fought for years alongside men; she had been a soldier of the regiment, and she had fought just as gallantly as any other soldier.

After she left the army, she fell upon hard times. Her friends petitioned the Duke of Cumberland to seek some help for her. After revealing her deception, I suppose she didn't qualify for any of the more usual forms of help. However, the Duke decided to be magnanimous, and granted her an annuity for life in recognition of her services to her country. Hannah Snell died in London in 1792, and is buried in Chelsea Hospital.

Wasperton

➤ Well and truly is Wasperton a hidden part of the county. Indeed, unless you happened to spot the fairly insignificant signpost on the main road between Barford and Wellesbourne, you would scarce know it existed.

It is an ancient parish and was once the property of Leofric, husband of the notable Lady Godiva of Coventry. It eventually passed through several hands coming at length to Dr Rawlinson, a somewhat secretive man, who kept a notebook relating to his Wasperton property. In 1736 he became involved with the restoration of the church there, which had been presented to the Bishop's Court for its bad state. Rawlinson was a bishop, consecrated in 1728 amid great secrecy. It seems secrecy was essential to him although there seems to have been no real need for it.

One John Morley was vicar here in the late 18th century, and kept a diary. It appears that William Welsh, also living in the parish, was a source of great bother to the vicar. Mr Welsh of Wasperton and Mr Lucy of Charlecote had something of an altercation in the local Wellesbourne inn, the Talbot, whereupon Mr Welsh appears to have given Mr Lucy a black eye. Rev Morley dined with Mr Lucy who was confined to his bed because of the black eye, and listened to his complaints against Mr Welsh. Rev Morley was asked to act as a go-between in order that good relations between the two men and their parishes might be restored.

Most of the old buildings, left by Dr Rawlinson to St John's College, Oxford, are now gone and upon their sites are built modern houses. The church of St John the Baptist was restored but not too heavily by Sir Gilbert Scott in the Gothick style which he loved, and the Victorian stained glass window is said to be to one of the last designs of Pugin.

But as recently as 1980-84, Wasperton was discovered to have a far greater treasure than any of these. Archaeologists digging in the gravel pits surrounding the parish came up with the Wasperton Hoard, now on permanent display at the County Museum. The digging had to be done expeditiously and with care, since the land was required for commercial purposes. It was decided that Wasperton must have been the site of an important Saxon settlement, since a large cemetery was discovered, with some 130 burials. The men had been interred with their weapons, and the women with their jewellery.

It seems the women of ancient Wasperton wore their brooches in pairs, called 'peplos', one on each shoulder to fasten their woollen garments. The brooches were made of bronze, probably melted down from Roman coins, and then gilded using mercury and amalgam. To some of them fibres still clung tenaciously. Archaeologists unearthed 66 brooches of ten different types dating from around AD 550. The work is beautiful, showing a great degree of artistry and sophistication.

Weethley

This very tiny, isolated and quite lonely spot, is now called Weethley Hamlet, as it says quite plainly on the gate you have to pass through to get right up to its highest point.

The name comes from the Anglo-Saxon meaning 'withywood' and from the lie of the land it is obvious that in ancient times there were more houses here than at present. Its population is increasing though. In 1911 it housed only 21 souls, whereas it now has some 33! Its few cottages, now well modernised, flank the lane, and one or two old buildings have been converted to form more houses.

It is quite extraordinary that such a tiny place should have a church at all, and yet it appears there has always been one here, even though there has never been any resident cleric, for Weethley has always been attached to another church, either Kinwarton, Alcester or Arrow.

In 1640, the historian Sir Simon Archer described the church at Weethley as 'buylded all of tymber, being half-tymbered both the chancell and the nave . . . there is both buriall and christning here . . . there are no armes or monuments . . .'. The old building he describes was replaced sometime before 1726, and the second plain brick structure may well have had a thatched roof.

In 1856 a man called Charles Jones wrote that the building contained no beauty or architectural merit, and was as devoid of ornament as any staunch puritan could desire. He said it was evidently the production of some homely knight of the 'pestle and mortar' living in the 18th century, and all he could find were a couple of ancient stone coffins buried in nettles!

However, about this time, Rev H. H. Miles took up the living at nearby Kinwarton, and his father, Mr Henry Miles, travelled from Herefordshire to visit his son in his new home. As he passed along the Ridgeway, he spotted the old church, now almost a ruin. Mr Henry Miles loved the site for indeed it was, and still is, very beautiful. He promptly offered to rebuild the church at Weethley at his own expense, an offer no one could refuse. The first stone was laid on 23rd May 1857, and beneath it the people of Weethley put new minted coins and other items of interest. Then they all had a party in a marquee erected on the site, and thanked Mr Miles in high fashion, for the rebuilding project cost that good man £1,500.

The church stands upon high ground, flanked by a lily pond with ducks happily paddling around upon it. The views across the plain, right over to the Cotswolds and as far as the Malvern hills, are superb, if slightly windy. They have a saying in Weethley 'If you can see the Malverns, it is going to rain. If you can't see them, it *is* raining'!

There are but a few gravestones within the tiny churchyard, and several of them lie gently above members of the Field family, who farmed here. One of the Fields, Ernest Frank, baptised in 1875, was a notable cricketer, and his photograph hangs in the county cricket ground at Edgbaston.

A service has been held every Sunday at Weethley, without interruption, since the turn of the century. Except in 1967, when the record was broken for six weeks because of an outbreak of Foot and Mouth disease upon the nearby farm. The only thing to do was to prevent anyone coming near, and consequently the church remained taboo. Fortunately, thanks to such measures, the farm was saved.

Wellesbourne

Nowadays, it would not be truthful to call Wellesbourne 'hidden'. It was once two very small villages, Wellesbourne Hastings and Wellesbourne Mountford, which came together at the river Dene, but over the past decade or so the village has expanded considerably and is now known simply as 'Wellesbourne'. However, despite the fact that the visitor may see Wellesbourne as a growing village of new developments, there are hidden corners and many stories well worth seeking out.

This part of Warwickshire was renowned for hunting, and many of the gentry built themselves hunting boxes, with ample stabling, where they and their servants spent the hunting season. The hunt kennels are still at Kineton, a couple of miles away. The house now known as Wellesbourne House was once called simply The Lodge, and was a hunting box built in 1819. It passed through several owners, each one putting his mark upon it, until in 1892 it was bought by William Low from Savannah, Georgia. A colourful character, who had been used to living the luxurious life of a Georgia plantation, Low immediately set about creating this kind of life in the small village of Wellesbourne. How it must have seemed to his neighbours, we do not know but it wasn't long before the gentry were clamouring for invitations, as did many notables including one or two Royal personages.

Clever William Low, who obviously had his priorities right, engaged a cook who rapidly built a reputation for Low's household and for herself at the same time. To dine at the Low table was to feast indeed, for his cook was no other than Rosa Lewis, a truly remarkable woman and a culinary artist par excellence. After Low's death in 1905, Rosa Lewis went on to become the colourful, down-to-earth owner of London's

Cavendish Hotel, later portrayed in the television series *The Duchess of Duke Street*. She was also the model for Lottie Crump in Evelyn Waugh's *Vile Bodies*.

Low, as one might expect, had the very first motor car in Wellesbourne, a 20 hp 19 cwt Golnon, and he had to build a special motor house in which to keep it. The motor house is now a private home.

His name is perpetuated in Lowes Lane which leads to where he once lived, the house which for a comparatively short time was the centre of Georgia plantation life in the small rural village of Wellesbourne. This house, still bearing traces of former glory, was requisitioned at the start of the Second World War, and used as WAAF billets. The land fairly close by was used to construct a war time airfield, and from it flew many of the unsung heroes of the war. Afterwards the house was bought by an industrialist, who set up a factory, which still exists.

Not far from Wellesbourne House, stands Wellesbourne Hall where the Dewes family lived for generations. Here too, for part of her life, lived Mrs Mary Delaney (1700-1788), sister of Mrs Dewes. Mary Delaney was a talented flower artist and friend of George III and his Queen Charlotte. Two of the shell decorated fireplaces in the house are her work. Indeed, several examples are to be found in the area, but many of her cut paper mosaics are to be found in the Victoria and Albert Museum in London. Eventually, the King granted her a small pension and she lived out her life in Windsor, the great friend of Fanny Burney.

Wellesbourne had a cricket club as early as 1824, although it was mainly for the gentry rather than the locals. It later moved to Warwick, but there are references in *Tom Brown's Schooldays* by Thomas Hughes to the famous Wellesbourne Match.

Just outside Wellesbourne is the site of Thelsford Priory, an ancient Trinitarian monastery, the first of its kind ever to be founded in this country. The friars who founded this house landed on these shores a whole decade before the Franciscans. Why they settled on Thelsford is not really known, but it is presumed it was because of the Lucy family at the great house of Charlecote, who gave them the land and continued to support them until the Dissolution of the Monasteries, when all of it went.

Not a stone of this once great priory remains on the site, but odd bits of it are to be found incorporated in many adjoining churches. Wellesbourne church acquired its bell.

Whatcote

This strangely haphazard hamlet is happily sited well off all main traffic routes. It is not on the way to or from anywhere in particular, and as such is able to remain fairly well hidden, except to those who deliberately seek it out.

The houses are mostly modern, and there is a fine old farm house. The village pond, well reeded, is often the chosen nesting place for a variety of water birds, including the Canada goose. There used to be a venerable row of old barns, but the changes in agriculture made them redundant and they are now converted to private homes.

The village is dominated by its local inn, the Royal Oak, standing four square and sturdy right in the centre. Solidly built of irregular blocks of local stone, with walls two ft thick in places, this is thought to be one of the oldest pubs in the country. The earliest part of the building dates back to 1168, and it is known to have been an ale house for more than eight centuries. It is doubtful whether it has always been called the Royal Oak, for that name only really came into popular use after King Charles II concealed himself in the Boscobel oak. Eight centuries ago, this pub would merely have hung a 'bush' outside. Or perhaps not even that, for didn't Shakespeare say 'Good wine needs no bush'?

The old pub sign swings gently to and fro above the door, and still bears the legend 'Chesham and Brackley Breweries Ltd' although this brewery has been out of existence now for many a long day. Legend has it that masons building the church at Whatcote first built the inn as a shelter, wherein they could live while work went on. Even after they had completed their work

The Royal Oak inn at Whatcote

and moved on to another job, this building still offered hospitality, it seems.

Certainly in 1642 after the Battle of Edgehill, which was not more than five miles off, weary soldiers fleeing from the skirmish paused at the ale house to slake their thirst. It is whispered that one of them was Oliver Cromwell, Old Noll himself, who had not at that time attained the notoriety that later came to him. The Parliamentarian forces used this building as a vantage point, and a good one it must have been, sitting as it does upon a crossroads. They even went so far as to order the removal of the bread oven so they could achieve an observation slit and look out down the road towards Edgehill without themselves being seen.

Longevity seems to be a fairly acceptable facet of life in Whatcote. The Royal Oak has survived more than 800 years. Inside the little Norman church is a memorial to John Davenport who died in 1668 at the ripe old age of 104 years. He held this living, and ministered to his Whatcote flock for more than 70 of those years, and while he remained a quiet parish priest, tucked well out of sight in Warwickshire, he must have heard the news of the death of Good Queen Bess; the return of Master Shakespeare, now famous, to live in Stratford; the Coronations of James I and Charles I; the Civil War, and the King's execution; the Commonwealth under Old Noll who once supped ale at Whatcote; the Restoration of the Monarchy and the triumph of Charles II; and the Great Fire of London, for all of these happened in the 70 years he lived in this tiny hamlet.

Whatcote is also known for two very strange customs. It is the last place in Warwickshire where 'rough music' was used. This is the custom that Thomas Hardy called the 'skimmety ride' in Dorset. It used to be quite widespread. When a man and a woman were found to be 'living in sin' without benefit of the Church, their neighbours let them know that it was not acceptable. They gathered together pots and pans, lids and pieces of metal, with which to make the 'rough music'. Standing outside the place where the guilty pair were living, they made as much noise as they could, meanwhile burning the couple in effigy. There would be much lewd shouting, and stones thrown at the door, so that the man and woman, whoever they were, would be left in no doubt of what their neighbours thought of their immorality. They usually left the place, secretly and at night.

Whatcote is also one of the last places to use a parish coffin and a parish burial sheet. The parish coffin was used to bury poor people and consisted of a moveable top and sides, so that the deceased would be carried to the churchyard in some style, then when the last of the mourners had departed, the top and sides would be removed to be used again, leaving the body, enshrouded, lying on a plain plank of wood. The burial sheet was left to the parish and consisted of a fine linen sheet with lace insertion which, when folded down, formed across. The bequest was that the sheet should only be used for single ladies of impeccable virtue.

Tiny and hidden though it is, Whatcote did suffer a dire blow during the Second World War. It was while Birmingham, some 30 or so miles off, was being steadily and regularly bombed. On 11th December 1940 there was a twelve hour air raid on the city of Birmingham, and a German bomber flying over Whatcote let fly a stick of eleven bombs right across the village. Most of them landed in fields and did little real harm. But one landed on the ancient church, and up flew most of the roof. The 15th century porch, part of the nave and the font were all destroyed, but the memorial to dear old John Davenport survived even this, as he had himself survived for 104 years. The church was restored in 1947, by local craftsmen, whose work is so true, you can honestly scarce see the join.

Whichford

Whichford is in the southernmost part of the county, and takes from the adjoining Cotswolds the undulating characteristics of the land and the mellow stone and mullions of its buildings. Its old stone cottages are widely spaced around a huge village green, rectangular in shape, upon which stands the old stone-built school, given by a local landowner in the 1850s. This remained virtually unaltered for more than a century, but despite protests from the residents, the school closed in 1985 and is converted into a house. Behind the school and the village green is the steep, well wooded rise of Whichford Hill, leading over the border into the county of Oxfordshire.

Whichford was a very early settlement and of some importance at one time, for it even had its own castle. Little remains now, though, except for a few earthworks, but the builders of it are commemorated within the church.

To the west of Whichford stands Whichford Wood, thought to be so ancient in origin as to be almost primeval. A steep bank runs through the wood, and there are the remains of fishponds. One part of the woodland is known as Fishponds Coppice, dating from the time when the monks of Bridlington owned it.

What is extraordinary about Whichford Wood is the Kitchener tree. Very difficult to find, its location is down an old track known as Doctor's Barn, named after a village doctor who did pretty well out of the Enclosure Act in the 19th century. Looking for a tree in a wood is even harder than finding a needle in a haystack. And the wood, despite its good management, or because of it, is very thick. The ground is always moist and muddy, and has never been turned.

The story is that a Corporal Ivens, home on leave in July 1916, was wandering in the wood. Many people wander in it; it is that kind of wood, and no matter how far or how long you wander, you never cross the same track twice, nor do you ever seem to meet anyone else. Young Corporal Ivens had just heard of the death of Kitchener of Khartoum on the HMS *Hampshire*, and it would appear that to Ivens he was something of a personal hero. Taking out his knife, without which no true countryman stirs from home, Corporal Ivens carved upon a young tree 'K of K. Drowned. 6.6.16. RIP'. Years passed, the tree grew, and so did the letters carved upon it, thus making a remote, truly hidden memorial in the most dense part of an ancient piece of Warwickshire woodland, in commemoration of a man who had become a nationally mourned hero.

Whichford belonged to the de Mohun family, of Norman origins, and they have a chapel in the church of St Michael, parts of which date from 1150. Within it is a tomb with an engrailed cross, to John de Mohun who died in the Scottish campaign of 1320. The last John de Mohun was one of the first Knights of the Garter, and when he died in 1376 he left no heirs, so Whichford passed to his youngest sister. But John had done a bit of spending in his time, and there wasn't much money left to maintain their various estates. The de Mohuns ceased to live at Whichford around 1405, and their castle was allowed to fall into a complete ruin.

The church has a small tomb recess which has aroused much speculation among experts. Some believe it to be the proposed burial place of a de Mohun infant; others say it is an Easter sepulchre which is rarely found in English churches. Truth to tell, no one really knows.

The most unusual monument is to a priest, John Mertun, rector of Whichford, 1507-1537. The top of the table tomb is covered with alabaster, and upon it is carved the figure of a priest in full vestments. Perhaps it is John himself. But what is unusual is that on the west end of the tomb is carved an open book, and beside it a pair of spectacles, the small round, metal rimmed ones. This is thought to be the first representation of reading glasses in England, so we may perhaps conclude that

John Mertun enjoyed reading, as befits a cleric, and was a bit short sighted. Spectacles were obviously available even in the early 16th century.

The church organ bears a brass plate telling us it was restored in 1927 by Lemuel A. Welles of New York, USA in memory of his ancestor Thomas Welles Govenor of Connecticut New England from 1655 to 1658. Thomas Welles came from Whichford, and ancient records contain many references to this name.

Whichford was one of the first villages to make some attempt at preventive medicine, for in 1783 there was a collection among the better off inhabitants to pay for inoculation against smallpox, and some £31 was raised to pay a Mrs Mackarness, a nurse and midwife who lived at Great Rollright, just up the hill. It is difficult to see what kind of inoculation was meant at this date, for Jenner was still working on his theories about smallpox, but perhaps Whichford was prepared to take any risks, realising how swiftly the disease could spread and its devastating effects.

Whitchurch

This is Bloom country, not the blossoms but the Rev J. Harvey Bloom, father of the novelist Ursula Bloom, who grew up here in the old rectory while her energetic father ministered to his flock.

The Norman church of St Mary can be spied right across the rather flat fields, from the main Stratford-upon-Avon to Shipston-on-Stour road, near the village of Alderminster. But to get anywhere near it you have to drive across a narrow field road, opening gates as you go, then turn half a mile or so down an old cart track. There is nothing much of Whitchurch now other than the church, surrounded by trees, with a barn and cottage nearby. The old rectory and a farmhouse still remain on the road that leads to Wimpstone.

Whitchurch is yet another of Warwickshire's depopulated villages, and the villain of the piece here is the same Edward

Belknap who pulled down the peasant's hovels and enclosed the common fields at Burton Dassett.

There was once an Anglo-Saxon settlement at Whitchurch, and the original church was almost certainly built of wood and thatch by the monks of Deerhurst in Gloucestershire, who owned much of the land roundabout. The church was rebuilt in the 11th century, and a bit of herringbone masonry on the north wall dates from this early period.

Rev J. Harvey Bloom achieved fame in Warwickshire long before his daughter began her career as a writer. He was a man of infinite energy, who appeared to be interested in everything and anything. He cycled all over the Midlands, taking notes upon many things; turned his attention to natural history; transcribed ecclesiastical records; did a complete survey of all the tombstones in Warwickshire churchyards, and for this we must needs be grateful to him for many of them have either disappeared or become totally illegible, as wind and weather have taken their toll.

As a naturalist he wrote of the plants, fossils and insects he discovered. He wrote regularly for the local paper, and produced learned papers for the Archaeological and Naturalist Societies. One of his most popular works was *Folklore in Shakespeare Land* published in 1930, which was reprinted in 1976. The Blooms were popular, and rapidly accepted into local society. Rev Bloom was a raconteur much in demand, and was regularly invited to take tea with Miss Marie Corelli, the novelist, who lived in Stratford-upon-Avon. This was indeed to be accepted, but he inevitably fell foul of that lady when he disagreed with her, and from then on he was snubbed by her. Not that it appears to have bothered him very much.

Whitchurch was noted for its ale brewing, and here it was said that two bushels of malt would produce:

> Forty gallons of clink-me-clear
> Forty gallons of table beer
> Forty gallons of Rat-me-Tat
> Forty gallons worse than that.

Neither Whitchurch, nor any of the hamlets adjoining it, had a pub. Consequently, to go out for a drink meant a very long walk across waterlogged fields, or an even longer walk by road, to the Bell at Alderminster. According to Ursula Bloom, writing of her childhood, this meant that no one bothered to go for just one drink, but having walked so far, went on a blind. The return journey was filled with hazard, and quite a few unfortunates did not manage to negotiate the unpredictable Stour. Every winter it claimed a victim. Rev Bloom offered free swimming lessons to all and sundry, but these were never taken up and his offer was regarded with some suspicion.

He was particularly incensed when a small boy fell into the water. Fortunately, the child's companion, a boy not much

The Crimscote Scold in Whitchurch church

older, showed great initiative. Grabbing the drowning child by one arm, the older boy clung with his other to the branch of a nearby tree and waited for help. He undoubtedly saved the younger child's life. Rev Bloom attempted to get him a Humane Society Medal, but waxed even more furious when told by the Society that as the rescuer hadn't actually gone into the river, and had scarce got his feet wet, he did not qualify!

The flat fields of Whitchurch flooded every winter, often turning into a sheet of water. On occasion, the flood rushing down from nearby Talton mill carried with it the odd dead sheep which would come to rest upon the flat lands, and would have to remain there, smelling atrociously, until the flood waters subsided enough to get anywhere near it.

Thankfully, this no longer happens. The river has been tamed, or at least as much as rivers can be tamed, and although the fields may get a bit muddy, they no longer disappear beneath the water.

Wilmcote

Perhaps the most famous of what have become known as the 'Shakespeare villages', Wilmcote was once the home of the great man's mother, Mary Arden. The old and very beautiful timbered farmhouse where she might well have been born, and where she certainly spent her childhood and formative years, now houses a museum of agricultural bygones, administered by the Shakespeare Birthplace Trust in Stratford-upon-Avon.

Robert Arden of Wilmcote had eight daughters and no sons. Mary married John Shakespeare, and he used some of her money to finance his undoubted business acumen. Robert Arden was well pleased with his son-in-law. In his will he left portions to each of his daughters, but by far the largest portion, which included property at Wilmcote then called 'Asbyes', to Mary Shakespeare, together with goods, cattle, bees and painted wall hangings. Mary and John Shakespeare lost two infant daughters before the birth of their first son, William, who was baptised in 1564. Even he might well have ended up beneath a tiny mound in the parish church, for only three months after his birth the plague came to Stratford-upon-Avon, carried by Leicester's soldiers returning from war in the Low Countries. Terrified, Mary Arden fled with her tiny son to take refuge at Wilmcote, and escaped the infection.

The Wilmcote property was at some stage in its life three cottages, and was not referred to as Mary Arden's House until 1789, long after Shakespeare and his contemporaries were dead and buried. The Trust obtained it in 1930 and have restored it perfectly, fitting it out with pieces of the period. As a result it is a magnet for tourists on the Shakespeare trail, and dominates this small village.

Wilmcote was a quarrying community in the 19th century and the lias stone, which is said to be of slightly 'doubtful' quality, was used to build many houses and to rebuild the great church of St Mary at Warwick when half of that town was destroyed by the Great Fire of Warwick in 1694.

Early in the 19th century an attempt was made to utilise the lower grade stone quarried from Wilmcote for cement. A few rows of small cottages were thrown up to house workers, and as a consequence the population of Wilmcote doubled almost overnight. The quarrymen, strangers to the place, had nothing to do in their spare time but get drunk in the Masons Arms, named because of the quarries, or alternatively take a cask or two home with them and get drunk there.

It seems during this period Wilmcote was a very sad place, with much drunkenness and poverty. Accordingly, the Knottesford-Fortescues, who were lords of the manor of Alveston, just outside Stratford-upon-Avon, decided to take a hand. Old Mr Fortescue was the typical kindly squire-parson, and because he did not want to send his youngest child, a son, away to school, had kept the young man beside him and intended him for the Church.

Wilmcote seemed a good place to start. There had once been a chapel here connected to the Guild of the Holy Cross in Stratford-upon-Avon, and a priest's house to go with it. The chapel had gone the way of all such small houses at the Dissolution, and the priest's house was a private home. All that really remained was a fine medieval pewter crucifix which had been dug up on the site of the old chapel.

The Knottesford-Fortescues selected carefully the site for a new church, St Andrew's, built in 1841 of blue lias, with Butterfield as its architect. The church was consecrated on St Martin's Day 1841, and Mr E.B. Fortescue was ordained as its very first priest-in-charge.

What was so unusual about this church is that it was the first in which full Catholic teaching and practice were restored after a lapse of 300 years. Eucharistic vestments were worn for the first time since the Reformation, and the set of vestments provided included superb 18th century examples of Festal Spanish and French purple. It was an Oxford Movement church. The early founders of the Movement – Newman, Pusey, Keble and Manning – were frequent visitors to Wilmcote, and although their published tracts against the 'Low Church' aroused much controversy, they must have discovered a truly kindred spirit in young Mr Knottesford Fortescue.

In 1845, Butterfield was requested to build a guest house here, one of his very first secular buildings. In this guest house was held the very first ever Retreat within the Church of England, attended by 40 priests and both Newman and Manning, who celebrated the occasion by planting a yew tree. Rev Knottesford Fortescue left Wilmcote in 1850, to be Provost of St Ninian's Cathedral, Perth.

Wixford

➤ This is the 'Papist Wixford' of the rhyme attributed to Shakespeare, although whether it did come from his quill is open to doubt. The jingle never saw the light of day until it appeared in a letter to the *Gentleman's Magazine* on 20th December 1794, when it was said to have been authenticated by a clergyman, a native of Warwickshire, who had died some 30 odd years before.

Why 'Papist' Wixford is a puzzle, and the only possible reason is because in Shakespeare's day the place belonged to the Throckmorton family who have lived for centuries at Coughton Court, just a few miles off. The Throckmortons have always been staunch adherents of the Catholic faith, and in the days of religious persecution they suffered for this. The very pleasant looking almshouses in Wixford were built by the Throckmortons in 1709 to house the poor.

The main part of the village is certainly not hidden, and its long curving street has three good pubs. The Three Horse Shoes dates in parts from the 17th century and was once next door to the village smithy, so that you could leave your horses to be dealt with while you nipped smartly next door to quench your thirst.

The ancient settlement was upon the site of an old ford, and as early as 1287 the monks of Bordesley had a fishery here. A bridge was mentioned in 1566, but the present bridge across the river Arrow is modern. Close to it upon the river bank is the appropriately named Fish Inn, and in the heyday of the railway, special excursion trains used to bring hundreds of anglers to enjoy themselves and their sport here.

What is really hidden in Wixford is the church, for if you did not know where to look it is unlikely that you would ever find it. It is tucked away at the top of a narrow high banked lane, the kind of lane that used to be so typical of Warwickshire. Even when you reach the top, you need to look about you, for inside the churchyard the oldest yew tree in the county almost obscures your first sight of the building.

The old tree's vast branches, some of them more than nine yards long, are propped up by crutches and interlace overhead. To stand beneath the tree is like being in a darkened room. This tree was the cause of a disagreement in 1669, when the priest, a Mr Kecke, announced his intention of cutting it down. The parishioners complained to the bishop about 'a certaine well growne yew tree in our churchyard of Wixford the like whereof is not to be found in all the diocese' and said they were indignant that he (Mr Kecke) should desire to 'deface ye churchyard of ye ornament' and asked the bishop to put a stop to such goings-on. Mr Kecke, equally indignant, protested against 'the false information of our papisticall parishioners . .

178

Priest's stable at Wixford

.'. But the bishop apparently stopped him for the yew tree remains.

Also in the churchyard, not far from the ancient yew, is a small, odd looking, thatched building of daub and wattle, believed to be 17th century in origin. It is faded, worn with use, and at first sight its purpose is obscure, as well it might be, for I think there is no other within the county. It is a stable, provided for the priest's horse. After the Reformation, Wixford no longer had a priest of its own, but had to share with the adjacent parish of Exall. Thus the priest had to ride hot foot between his two parishes, and needed a stable to house his weary steed while he conducted services inside the church.

Visitors come to the lovely church of St Milburga at Wixford to see the Cruwe brass, dating from 1411 and quite the best of its kind anywhere in the Midlands. It is five ft long, complete with inscriptions, and lies upon the top of a tomb in the south chapel, built by Cruwe in 1400. Thomas Cruwe is wearing armour, his wife a rich gown and mantel, and surrounding them are bare feet, 52 of them. The brass is quite perfect and those studying costume of this period have found it invaluable.

Thomas de Cruwe was steward and legal adviser to Margaret Beauchamp, Countess of Warwick, and this could have been no easy task during the troublous times of King Richard II and Henry IV. But he appears to have managed the job quietly and efficiently, since very little is known of him, except for the chapel he built here, and his truly magnificent brass. He married Julian, widow of Sir John Clopton, who owned lands at Wixford.

There is a curious legend that Wixford was the scene of the death of the patron saint of England, St George. After he had killed the dragon in Coventry, of course! He is supposed to have been buried in Wixford at a crossroads, with a stake driven through his heart, and from this stake grew a superb giant of an elm tree. Should the bark of this tree be cut, then it oozed blood, the life blood of the saint himself.

In the 1930s, F.W. Bennett, author of *Tiddyoody Pie* went to see for himself if there was any truth in the matter. He did cut the bark of the elm, and reported that it oozed sap of a rusty red colour. He decided that although the tree did not mark the last resting place of our good St George, it might well mark a suicide's grave, as was so often the custom in earlier times. Suicides could not be buried in consecrated ground. They had committed the worst sin of all, self murder, and it was therefore considered right and proper they should be buried where roads crossed in order that all travellers should walk upon their grave and thus add to the dishonour. A stake was often driven through the heart in order to anchor the unquiet spirit, so that it should not walk abroad.

The old elm tree grew older, so that it became quite hollow in the middle. An ideal place for children to play, to make dens. Sometime in the 1950s, children playing around inside the old tree started a fire; the tree caught, and was so badly damaged that its charred remains had to be felled. The lane where the tree once stood is still called George's Elm Lane, as it always has been. No one has come up with any theories about why St George, who was supposed to be in the Holy Land with the Crusaders, should have come to tiny Wixford.

Wood Bevington

This place is so well hidden it scarcely exists. It is one of the many places in Warwickshire that became depopulated, and in this case it was caused by Thomas Grey in 1506. Together with its neighbour, Cock Bevington, it used to belong to the Abbot of Evesham, and comes within the confines of the parish of Salford Priors.

The Bevingtons remained something of a waste; indeed they used to be called Bevington Waste, but in the early 1870s a gang of men working for four years turned 400 acres to productive agriculture. The foreman of the gang, Arthur Allchurch, who lived near Evesham, commemorated the completion of their task by writing a song called *The Wake of Bevington* to the well known tune of *Auld Lang Syne*. It begins:

> Come all you jolly labouring men and listen to my song
> The theme is well known to you all, it is of Bevington
> Five years ago great oaks did grow, mid thorns and
> briars long
> But now the labouring men have made cornfields of
> Bevington.

There are several verses. One describes how 'Mr Webb' stood treat when the work was done, and how two men, 'Boots and Booker', had a fight at the 'Wake of Bevington'.

But long before this, in the old manor house at Wood Bevington, there lived Father Joachim, a priest on the run. His real name was John Wall, and he was born in Lancashire in 1620. He went to Douai to become a priest and eventually became Father Vicar and Instructor of Novices. In 1656 he was sent to

181

England, and made his way to the manor house at Wood Bevington, where he was responsible for the Catholics throughout Warwickshire and the Midlands. They were dreadful times. John Wall used many names and disguises to go about his work, and the one by which he was best known was Father Joachim.

Many of the Catholic houses had priest's hiding holes, for the mass was forbidden. One of Father Joachim's stopping places was Harvington Hall near Worcester, a house which contains no less than eleven priest holes. He almost certainly spent a night or two in some of them. Eventually though, he was captured, at the time when an the country was up in arms over the fictitious Titus Oates plot against the Protestant religion. Father Joachim was found, arrested and flung into gaol in Worcester Castle.

He was found guilty of treason, although his only offence seems to have been to celebrate the mass of his faith. He suffered the dreadful death common to what the state was pleased to call traitors. He was hanged, drawn and quartered at Red Hill, Worcester, on 22nd August 1679. Because he was martyred for his faith, Blessed St John Wall was canonised on 25th October 1970.

There is no memorial of his work at Wood Bevington, but a bronze relief showing him surrounded by geese, ducks, a wagtail, a dove, sparrow and nuthatch, all birds still remaining at Harvington Hall, hangs in the Catholic church there.

Wormleighton

Set in fairly flat land, with only the slightest undulations, Wormleighton is one of Warwickshire's depopulated villages, and yet appears to have survived remarkably well and in the process achieved an enviable degree of serenity. It lies on the top of a low hill and only a mile off stands the Three Shires Stone marking the spot where the boundaries of Warwickshire, Northamptonshire and Oxfordshire meet.

The Oxford canal was constructed through here in 1778, a flat and pleasant stretch of gentle water, more like a meandering river than a feat of engineering skill. Close to it are the mounds and hollows of the old deserted village.

In the centre of this pleasant village, consisting now of one street and a scattering of estate-style cottages, stands the old manor house built by the Spencer family, whose main seat was at Althorp in Northamptonshire, just across the border.

The depopulation was begun by William Cope, cofferer to King Henry VII, who enclosed 240 acres of land here and in one stroke rendered homeless the occupants to twelve messuages and three cottages. In 1507, Cope sold Wormleighton to John Spencer who promptly began to build his grand manor house, suitable to accommodate his entire household of 60 persons and to mark the rise in his fortune and status. He was a great benefactor to the church, but he too enclosed land for the better rearing of sheep, since it was in the wool trade riches were seen to lie. His descendant Robert was created Baron Spencer of Wormleighton in 1603, shortly after King James I came to the throne.

The Spencers continued building as the years went on, and the old manor house was among the finest in the country. It was originally built to form an open quadrangle, with the shields and heraldic emblems of the Spencers (Dieu Defend le Droit) and their appropriate marriage connections. One particularly beautiful room is the Star Chamber where the panelling and lintels are decorated with gilt stars. In 1613 Robert Spencer built the handsome gatehouse, with its superb archway, and on the south front the Royal Arms.

There were many illustrious visitors to the old manor house at Wormleighton in its heyday. In 1571 Robert Dudley, Earl of Leicester, with a vast retinue of servants and notables, stayed here as guests of Spencers. The following year, the quiet old manor house was once more a-bustle, ready to welcome Queen Elizabeth I who was making something of a progress through rural Warwickshire.

Then came the Civil War, setting brother against brother, friend against friend, and although the Spencers kept a low profile, Prince Rupert chose to make Wormleighton his battle headquarters. It was from this old house he rode out at the head of his troop on that bitterly cold morning of 23rd October 1642, to fight at the side of his uncle, King Charles I, at the Battle of Edgehill.

It was the Civil War that put an end to the grandeur of the old manor house, for in January 1646, Royalist forces rode into Wormleighton and set the old house ablaze to prevent it falling into Parliamentarian hands. It never recovered. What remains of the old house, and this is still very beautiful, is now a working farm. The gatehouse remains, and beyond it can be seen the church, approached down a quiet, narrow leafy lane. Geese peck around in front of the church door, and few if any cars venture this far, since it leads on to nowhere.

Inside the church is a handsome memorial to John, son and heir of Robert the first Lord Spencer of Wormleighton, who died in Blois, France in the year 1610, aged '19 years, eight months and odd dayes'. Under a circular stone close by are buried the 'bowells' of Robert, Lord Spencer, his father, who died in 1627. It was a fairly common practice in important families for the viscera to be buried in one family church, whilst the rest of the body was taken off to be buried in another, each place being closely connected with the dead person's estate.

It was here at Wormleighton that Robert, Lord Spencer, began the famous collection of books that formed the foundation of the Spencer Library, now transferred to the John Rylands Library in Manchester.

There is one family who lived here in Wormleighton who have left no trace, not even the smallest memorial within the church, merely the entries in the parish registers. Robert Washington, second son of Robert Washington of Sulgrave, just a few miles away, was married in Wormleighton church to Elizabeth Chishull on 19th February 1595. Elizabeth was a local girl. Robert Washington's brother, Lawrence, also lived here and his son, George Washington, was baptised at Wormleighton on 3rd August 1608. Later both Lawrence and his brother Robert moved to live in Brington in Northamptonshire, and this Lawrence Washington is the direct ancestor of the George Washington who became the first President of the United States in 1789.

Wroxall

Initially, it may appear that there is little within the hamlet for the casual visitor, but just a little way off stands Wroxall Abbey, a Victorian mansion which replaced the wonderful old Elizabethan house. It is now a private girls school, and within its precincts stand the ruins of a 12th century Benedictine nunnery, with close by the parish church of St Leonard.

Wroxall was given to Henry de Newburgh, first Earl of Warwick, just after the Conquest, and was later possessed by Richard de Hatton, who had a son, Hugh. This Hugh was a strong man of larger than usual physical stature, and being filled with a desire for adventure he went to fight in the Holy Land. Adventure he probably had, but things didn't quite work out according to plan, for Sir Hugh was captured and imprisoned. It seems he was kept in dreadful conditions, and underwent many privations for seven long years, during which time he thought constantly of his home at Wroxall and prayed for deliverance.

He recalled that his own parish church was dedicated to St Leonard and accordingly addressed his prayers to this saint. One night St Leonard, clad in the habit of a black monk, appeared to Sir Hugh in his noisome cell, telling him to go home and found upon his land a nunnery dedicated to St Benedict. When Sir Hugh awoke, he merely thought he had been dreaming.

The following night, St Leonard once again appeared to Sir Hugh, repeating his command that a Benedictine nunnery should be founded at Wroxall. Sir Hugh asked how he could do anything about it, since he was a prisoner, kept in chains? St Leonard said that upon Sir Hugh taking a solemn vow, he would be delivered. After seven long years, Sir Hugh gladly made the solemn vow to found the nunnery, and no sooner were the words out of his mouth, than he discovered himself, still with the chains about his wrists, and clad in torn and lice ridden rags, wandering around his own woodlands at home at Wroxall.

He was spotted by a loitering shepherd, who was frightened at first by his appearance and failed to recognise his master in this gaunt, filthy stranger, with seven years' growth of hair and beard matted about his head and face. Eventually Sir Hugh calmed his fears and convinced him that he was indeed his lord returned from the dead. He asked him to break the news to his wife and children so that they would not be frightened when he appeared, and the shepherd ran off.

Then hurrying post haste appeared the Lady Hugh, wimple all awry, but she too failed to recognise her lord. It was not until he had ferretted around in his rags and brought forth his half of a ring they had broken together when he left for the Crusade, and she was able to fit it to her half which she kept always with her, that she believed him. Together they knelt down upon the ground and gave grateful thanks for his deliverance. St Leonard appeared for the last time to Sir Hugh, and told him that the exact spot where he wished the nunnery to stand would be marked by stones the following day.

It was so. The following morning, the stones had been pushed into the ground to mark the area, and Sir Hugh kept his vow and built the nunnery. He gave much of his money towards its upkeep, and two of his daughters became nuns within it. The nunnery lasted for many years, and was eventually dissolved in 1536 when Henry VIII was busy closing down all small religious houses. The nuns were turned out and 'exposed to the wide world' to make their own way as best they might.

The date of the second miracle of Wroxhall is not exactly known, but is likely to have been between the years 1135 and 1284. It concerns one of the nuns, Dame Alice Craft, a 'Ladye' of Wroxall described as being rich in virtues but poor in worldly goods. What Dame Alice had set her heart upon was a chapel dedicated to Our Lady, attached to the priory church of St Leonard. She prayed regularly that this might happen, until one night Our Lady appeared before her as she knelt at prayer, and in effect told her to get on with the job!

Dame Alice wonderingly asked how could she build a chapel when she had no money. Our Lady appeared a second time and told her to have faith, for she would always have just enough money to pay the workmen for their weeks labour until the chapel was completed. 'Where must the chapel stand?' asked the quavering Dame Alice, and was told this would be made perfectly plain to her if she kept her eyes and ears open.

According to the old legend, it was around harvest time, therefore warm and sunny, when one morning Dame Alice went out to the church very early. To her astonishment she found a patch of ground on the north side of the church covered with snow. It was a perfect rectangle, as if it had been carefully drawn. The rest of the land and garden all round it was still blooming and burgeoning with summer grasses and wild flowers. The snow remained upon this patch until noon of that day, and Dame Alice called in masons to mark off the area, for she knew this was where she must build the chapel of Our Lady.

She regularly prayed for help and guidance, and regularly every Saturday she was able to gather enough silver coins from the churchyard paths where they miraculously appeared, to pay the masons for their week's labour. There was never a coin short or a coin left over! The chapel was eventually complete, and Dame Alice seeing her work accomplished, died. She was buried before the door of her chapel, and some years later when restoration work caused her bones to be disturbed, it was found that she, like Sir Hugh, was of larger than usual stature.

Wroxall passed through many hands until 1713 when it was bought by the great architect, Sir Christopher Wren. The Wren family had originated from Warwickshire centuries before, and when Christopher Wren's son married a widow of the family of Burgoyne, the famous man obviously decided it was time for the family to come back to their roots and settle in Warwickshire; so he bought Wroxall as a home for the newly married pair.

He himself enjoyed staying there in the next ten years, during which time he built a few unusual features in the extensive and very beautiful gardens, designed a few unusual curving brick walls to form wind breaks and give shelter, entertained hugely and was convivial company, before his own death in 1723.

Sad to say then that the old house which had seen so much eventually fell victim to Victorian vandalism, and was pulled down by a rich merchant from Liverpool. The present Victorian Tudor mansion was built in its stead in 1864 and is typical of the substantial style of that period.

Bibliography:

Warwickshire (Hickman 1979)
Highways & Byways in Shakespeare Country (Hutton 1914)
Tiddyoody Pie (F W Bennett 1930)
Bygone Warwickshire (Andrews 1893)
Rambles in Shakespeare Country (Wade 1932)
Haunted Warwickshire (Atkins 1981)
Antiquities of Warwickshire (Dugdale)
Historic Warwickshire (Burgess 1893)
Shakespeare Land (Ribton-Turner 1893)
Folklore and Superstition in Shakespeareland (Bloom 1929)
Warwickshire (Lisle 1936)
Warwickshire Villages (Cave 1977)
Rambles Round the Edgehills (Miller 1967 Reprint)
Rosemary for Stratford on Avon (Bloom 1966)
Warwickshire (Alan Burgess 1950)
Warwickshire (Bird 1973)
Old Warwickshire Families and Houses (Burman 1934)
Lives of the Queens of England (Strickland 1882)
Catholic Brailes (Suffolk)
Warwickshire (Mee 1936)
Unknown Warwickshire (Dormer Harris 1924)
Folklore of Warwickshire (Palmer 1976)

Plus, of course, many back copies of local newspapers, including the Stratford-on-Avon Herald, Evesham Journal, Leamington Courier, Focus magazine, and others.

Index